SECURITY & HUMAN ASPECTS

Educational Resources

Bruno Ciroussel

COPERNICUS IP

Cover Graphics: Copernicus IP

First edition: February 2024

© 2024, Bruno Ciroussel Copernicus IP, USA

ISBN: 978-2-3225-0426-8

Copernicus IP

2915 OGLETOWN
ROAD, #4402 NEWARK,
DE 19713 USA

Édition : BoD - Books on Demand, info@bod.fr
Impression : BoD – Books on Demand,
In de Tarpen 42, Norderstedt (Allemagne)
Impression à la demande
Dépôt légal : Mars 2024

TABLE OF CONTENTS

OPENING

"In a single moment, the energetic essence of the entire universe is unveiled."

After 15 years of extensive research and development, I am thrilled to present my book, "Innovation Unleashed: Manual AITEK 6," now available in bookstores. Within its pages, I delve deeply into the intricate concepts of my groundbreaking machine learning platform. This platform is distinguished by its innovative use of Auto-ML, its proprietary vector base, its automated process management system, and its insightful predictive dashboards. Additionally, I introduce the integration of business solutions known as knowledge cartridges, further enhancing its capabilities.

Between 2002 and 2006, alongside the creation of Aitek, I had the privilege of teaching security and human factors at the "Institut de lutte contre la criminalité économique"

(ILCE) in Neuchâtel. The material developed for my teaching has evolved into a book, now accessible on Amazon. This journey has allowed me to share my insights into the challenges of computer security and human interaction within this realm with a broader audience — an enriching experience indeed.

In my relentless pursuit of societal innovation, I have harnessed this extraordinary platform to delve into the intersection of direct democracy and artificial intelligence. My essay, accessible on Amazon, offers a compelling exploration of the transformative possibilities arising from this amalgamation.

Venturing beyond the conventional boundaries of exploration, I immerse myself in an imaginative odyssey set in a dystopian universe within the science fiction genre. My novel, "*L'espace d'un instant,*" takes Society to its darkest limits, exploring potential deviations and unravelling the complexities and challenges that emerge when my platform and AI encounter formidable circumstances.

INTRODUCTION

"If you know neither your enemies nor yourself, you will know your battles by your defeats" (The Art of War, Sun Tzu 600 BC)"

I am pleased to present this document, representing the course I delivered at the Institute for the Fight against Economic Crime (ILCE in french) in Neuchâtel from 2001 to 2006. This period marked a fascinating chapter in my career, with a dual focus on academic instruction and the pivotal design phase of my artificial intelligence and big data plat-form, Aitek.

During this time, the platform was still in its formative stages. While dedicating part of my time to academic teaching, we were concurrently developing the alpha version of the Aitek platform. Simultaneously, we laid the groundwork for the "knowledge cartridges" in various sectors such as pharmaceuticals, retail, customs, and supply chain, setting the stage for their future development.

When we were conducting oral exams for our students, Cedric and I came up with the idea of developing a knowledge cartridge for an Intelligent SOC (Security Operation Center) for cybersecurity. We worked together to design this innovation. I still remember a photo we took at Société Ilion after presenting our project to the team. It was an exciting moment when we could see our work taking shape.

Regrettably, Cedric's unexpected departure abruptly halted the project, and the knowledge cartridge remained dormant until now. I have undertaken the task of revisiting and organizing my notes from that period, forming Part II of my ongoing work. After necessary refinement and updates to these notes, I embarked on the writing of Part II.

In acknowledgment of their pivotal roles in this experience, I dedicate this course to two individuals who significantly contributed to its development.

I extend my sincere appreciation to Isabelle Augsburger-Bucheli, the dean of the institute, for her trust in assigning me this responsibility. Her steadfast support and expertise have been a continual source of inspiration throughout my tenure as an educator. It is under her guidance that I have been able to grow and contribute modestly to the institute.

In addition, I dedicate this course to Cédric Renouard, my collaborator for practical work and exams. Although Cédric departed too soon, entering the realm of geeks, his keen intellect, passion for technology and cybersecurity, and his eagerness to share knowledge have left an indelible mark on my professional journey.

This course (Part I) reflects my collaboration with the course I've had the pleasure of teaching for computer security education and awareness in the fight against economic crime. I trust that this document will continue to be a valuable resource for new students and professionals entering this field.

I express my gratitude to all of you for your support and contributions to our shared mission. It is through the efforts of dedicated colleagues that we can truly make a difference in the ongoing battle against economic crime.

PART 1:
IT SECURITY AND
HUMAN FACTORS

"Life is a web woven by humans, where randomness is the thread that creates unpredictable patterns."

CHAPTER 1.0: COMPUTER SECURITY AND ECONOMIC CRIME

"The why is the door that opens the path to knowledge."

IT security plays a crucial role in the fight against economic crime. With the rapid advancement of technology and the increasing digitization of business activities, cybercriminals are increasingly exploiting the vulnerabilities of computer systems to commit acts of fraud, theft of sensitive information and sabotage.

Strong IT security is essential to prevent and detect cyber-criminal attacks, protect confidential data, and maintain the integrity of an organization's IT systems. Here are just a few reasons why IT security is important in the fight against economic crime:

Protecting Sensitive Data: Companies handle extensive amounts of sensitive data, encompassing financial information, personal customer data, and trade secrets. A security breach can result in severe consequences, including identity theft, financial fraud, and a loss of customer trust. Robust IT security measures are crucial to safeguarding this sensitive data and mitigating the risk of compromise.

Preventing Phishing Attacks: Cybercriminals often employ phishing techniques to deceive users into disclosing confidential information, such as login credentials or passwords. Effective IT security involves preventative measures and awareness campaigns to thwart phishing attacks and shield users from fraudulent attempts.

Intrusion Detection and Response: Effective IT security involves the implementation of intrusion detection and real-time monitoring systems to promptly identify suspicious activities on networks and systems. Early detection enables swift action to limit potential damage and minimize operational disruption.

Financial Transaction Security: As online financial transactions become more common, it is crucial to protect these transactions against fraud attacks. Strong IT security ensures the integrity of financial transactions by implementing encryption protocols, robust authentication mechanisms, and fraud detection systems.

Preserving Reputation and Trust: Companies falling victim to cybercrime attacks risk significant damage to their reputation and customer trust. Robust IT security demonstrates a commitment to protecting customer data, thereby strengthening trust and loyalty.

Regulatory Compliance: government and industry regulations mandate companies to protect sensitive information and implement appropriate security measures. Strong IT security facilitates compliance, avoiding penalties and legal disputes associated with non-compliance.

In conclusion, robust IT security is a pivotal element in the fight against economic crime. It safeguards sensitive data, prevents phishing attacks, detects intrusions, secures financial transactions, preserves reputation, and ensures regulatory compliance. Organizations prioritizing IT security enhance their ability to counter cyber threats and safeguard economic interests. The Master's program, while not exclusively focused on technology, recognizes the significance of IT security in combating economic crime. Students gain essential technological insights to understand negligence, ignorance, and embezzlement issues in this context.

The program emphasizes the importance of strong IT security, playing a vital role in the fight against economic crime. The program acknowledges technological advances creating opportunities for criminals and disrupting economic activities. Students learn about computer security concepts, best practices, and the implementation of technical, organizational, and human measures to protect IT systems, sensitive data, and critical processes.

Understanding potential threats and techniques used by economic criminals, students actively contribute to developing and implementing sound security strategies. They can advise organizations on asset protection, prevent data leakage, detect suspicious activity, and respond effectively to incidents.

Moreover, the program underscores cooperation and collaboration between professionals from diverse fields, including accountants, law enforcement agencies, and the judiciary. Combating economic crime demands a multidisciplinary approach where technology plays a central role. Students learn to work collaboratively, solving complex problems, sharing information, and coordinating efforts to prevent and suppress economic crime.

In summary, the Master's degree provides students with a comprehensive understanding of strong IT security and its crucial role in countering economic crime. They gain knowledge and skills to analyse risks, implement effective security strategies, and contribute to protecting companies and systems against emerging threats.

CHAPTER 1.1: APPROACH AND DEFINITION

"Words are vessels navigating the vast sea of meaning, voyaging bet-ween the shores of comprehension and the abysses of incom-prehension."

When discussing computer security, the conversation often centers around hacking, carried out by various categories of hackers. There are "white hat" hackers, contracted to identify and rectify security vulnerabilities. Then, there are "grey hats" who discover flaws without being contracted but work to fix them without causing harm. Finally, there are "black hats" who exploit vulnerabilities for personal gain, disregarding the potential consequences.

These skills necessitate a deep understanding of electronics and advanced computer science. To illustrate, here are a few examples presented in a way that's accessible to the general public, avoiding technical details to prevent any potential replication of these operations.

Example 1: Where's my car?

Information technology (IT) has become pervasive across all sectors, including modern vehicles. To illustrate, let's explore how one could manipulate a modern car without its key. This scenario involves the internal communication bus known as the CAN Bus, developed in 1985 and standardized in 1991 (ISO 11898-2:2003). The CAN Bus manages exchanges between various components of vehicles, providing diagnostics on aspects like tire status, headlight status, brake status, emission control, key presence, etc.

While external communication with the vehicle is typically well secured, internal communication through the CAN Bus is often unencrypted. With a basic microcontroller, a battery, a few lines of assembly language, and proper connectors, one could connect a device to the headlights. This connected device, recognized as an internal element, can then send a series of messages amid a chaotic situation (similar to a DDoS attack) and signal the presence of the key.

With the vehicle falsely convinced that the key is present, the attacker can open the door and drive away, though caution is advised on the road (as certain functionalities like headlights may not operate optimally).

An essential detail often overlooked is that, in approximately 67% of cases, the vehicle registration document is stored in the glove compartment. While we cannot completely prevent sophisticated exploitation by malicious individuals, adopting simple habits, such as avoiding leaving important documents inside the vehicle, can make their task more challenging.

It's crucial to note that, as of your reading this, manufacturers have likely implemented measures to address such vulnerabilities. The security of electronic systems is continuously advancing to counter potential flaws and safeguard users from unauthorized manipulations. Industries responsible for these technologies incorporate protection mechanisms and regular updates to ensure a higher level of security and prevent intrusions.

Example 2: A few clock strokes later...

The internal architecture of a computer system relies on periodic interrupts generated by a clock. These interrupts occur at regular intervals, synchronized with the system's internal clock. Each interrupt prompts the processor to temporarily halt its normal execution flow, allowing for the management of tasks or the execution of specific routines.

Consider a microprocessor operating on an internal clock. At predefined intervals, this clock triggers an interrupt, commonly referred to as a clock interrupt. This initiates a coordinating routine, which varies based on the operating system running on the microprocessor. Operating systems like Windows, Unix/Linux, or macOS, for instance, use this interrupt to initiate a task scheduling process. This process involves reorganizing pending tasks and determining which tasks should be executed based on factors like priority and current status.

An example of such an interrupt is 1Ch, known as the clock tick, a periodic BIOS (Basic Input/Output System) interrupt occurring with each pulse of the computer's internal clock. On Intel x86 systems, this interrupt is addressed via the 1Ch interrupt vector. It activates approximately every 54.9254 milliseconds, with a frequency of around 18.2064819336 times per second, dependent on the internal clock frequency. During this interrupt, the processor temporarily suspends the normal execution of the ongoing program to perform a service or function related to time management.

Interrupt handling is a technique commonly used to modify or extend the standard behaviour of a computer system. By redirecting an interrupt to its own code, a program can intervene in the system's regular execution flow and execute specific actions, such as modifying parameters, executing custom code, or redirecting the interrupt back to the original routine to maintain normal system flow.

However, interrupt handling demands a deep understanding of both hardware and software, with precautions necessary to ensure system stability and security. For a malicious user to install this type of software, gaining access to the PC or phone is crucial. The human factor remains a critical element of protection even in this context, emphasizing the importance of addressing vulnerabilities related to user behaviour.

The examples provided showcase the breadth of possibilities, requiring expertise and knowledge beyond the scope of students in this course. Such topics are better suited for experts with continuous updates on a wide range of technologies, as individuals often pose the weakest link in IT security.

I could also include an example, for instance, demonstrating how one might gain access to a mailbox with knowledge of the phone number through social engineering. By employing a phone key simulator and a brute-force method, one could attempt to access the phone's voicemail and retrieve the new password.

While the use of phone key simulators was more prevalent in the past, it's crucial to clarify that this example is not intended as a hacking tutorial. Instead, it highlights a potential vulnerability where users (the human factor) may succumb to social engineering tactics. Social engineering involves the psychological manipulation of individuals to acquire confidential information or prompt specific actions. In this relatively simplistic example, the method of retrieving a mailbox using a phone number and a ringtone generator illustrates a social engineering strategy aimed at obtaining personal data.

Understanding the security risks associated with human behaviour, whether unintentional, induced, or malicious, is essential. The primary objective is to foster an appropriate approach among individuals to guard against these risks by providing a comprehensive understanding of their IT environment. The focus is on raising awareness of potential threats, teaching individuals how to identify, prevent, and protect themselves against these dangers, while leaving the technical aspects to the experts. This approach aims to equip individuals with the necessary reflexes to navigate securely in a world where cybersecurity risks are pervasive.

This course's goal is to explore the impact of the human factor in computer security and trace the flow of information through its traces. It does not intend to teach security administration, hacking, or the technical use of trace management tools. The emphasis will be on a conceptual and logical understanding.

Firstly, we will seek to understand what an information flow is, the role of computer security, and the importance of the time factor. Then, we will define human behaviour and explore the concepts of risk and error, addressing risky behaviours and cybercrime.

Once these concepts are grasped, we will delve into security measures such as prevention, detection, protection, and insurance. In the context of detection, we will tackle the delicate subject of traces and logs, as detection requires the use of these elements.

Finally, we will explore the relationship between individuals and security, concluding with ethical considerations. Throughout this course, the focus will be on understanding the interaction between human factors and security and how they mutually influence each other. By studying these concepts, the aim is to deepen the understanding of complex dynamics in the field of information security.

It is important to note that this course aims to provide a conceptual foundation and encourage critical thinking in the field of security rather than impart practical skills or technical expertise.

We hope this course will provide you with valuable insights into the human factor in security. The challenges of computer security related to the human factor are numerous and significant, requiring special attention to minimize risks associated with errors and negligent behaviours of individuals. Here are some key elements to consider:

Awareness and Training: It is crucial to raise employees' awareness of the risks associated with computer security and train them on best practices. This includes protecting confidential information, managing passwords, recognizing phishing attacks, and social engineering techniques. Adequate awareness enables employees to be aware of potential threats and actively contribute to the organization's security.

Social Engineering: Attackers often use social engineering techniques to exploit individuals' trust and obtain sensitive information. Employees must be aware of tactics such as phishing, spear-phishing, and fraudulent calls. By understanding the signs of a social engineering attempt, employees are better prepared to identify and avoid these attacks.

Access Management: Human errors related to access management can lead to unauthorized access to systems and sensitive data. It is essential to implement strict access management policies, including the use of strong passwords, two-factor authentication, and limiting permissions to only those who need them. Proper access management significantly reduces risks associated with the human factor.

Mobile Device Management: With the proliferation of mobile devices in professional environments, it is imperative to educate employees about the risks associated with their use. Security policies should include measures such as device password protection, data encryption, and awareness of malicious applications. By adopting secure practices, employees contribute to the protection of company data.

Excessive Privileges: Employees with excessive access privileges can pose a significant security risk. It is crucial to implement appropriate controls to limit privileges to those who truly need them to perform their tasks. Following the principle of least privilege, organizations reduce the risks of abuse or unauthorized access.

Incident Management: Swift and appropriate response to security incidents is essential to minimize potential damage. Employees should be trained on procedures in case of incidents, such as detecting and reporting suspicious activities, preserving evidence, and communicating with IT security teams. Effective incident management helps contain security breaches and reduces their impact.

Security Culture: a strong security culture is fundamental to promoting responsible behaviours in computer security. Employees should be encouraged to report incidents, share their concerns, and actively participate in the organization's security efforts. A well-established security culture reinforces collective vigilance and fosters a proactive attitude towards data protection.

Computer security is a shared responsibility between IT security teams and all members of the organization. By recognizing the importance of the human factor and investing in awareness, training, and building a security culture, organizations can reduce risks associated with errors and negligent behaviours, thereby strengthening their overall security posture.

"Computer security" encompasses several realities that are good to discern before embarking on our journey. The flow of information represents the movement of data within a computer system, including information acquisition, storage, communication, and processing. Understanding this flow is essential for grasping the challenges of computer security.

Computer security aims to ensure the integrity, durability, and availability of attributes within the information flow. This includes protection against threats such as intrusions, viruses, denial-of-service attacks, as well as the preservation of data confidentiality. By implementing appropriate security measures, the goal is to prevent security incidents and limit potential damages.

Confidentiality is a crucial aspect of computer security, ensuring that only authorized individuals have access to the information flow within the operating system. This may involve the use of encryption mechanisms, strict access controls, and policies for managing confidential data.

Time is an important factor not to be neglected in computer security. Information systems evolve constantly, emerging threats multiply, and security needs change. Therefore, proactive security management, regular audits, adherence to best practices, and staying updated on the latest technological advancements and known vulnerabilities are paramount.

What we commonly refer to as "computer security" encompasses all aspects related to the protection and confidentiality of the computerized information flow over time. It is a constantly evolving field that requires continuous vigilance and adaptation to new threats and technologies.

By exploring these concepts, we can better understand the challenges of computer security and be able to implement appropriate measures to protect our systems and data.

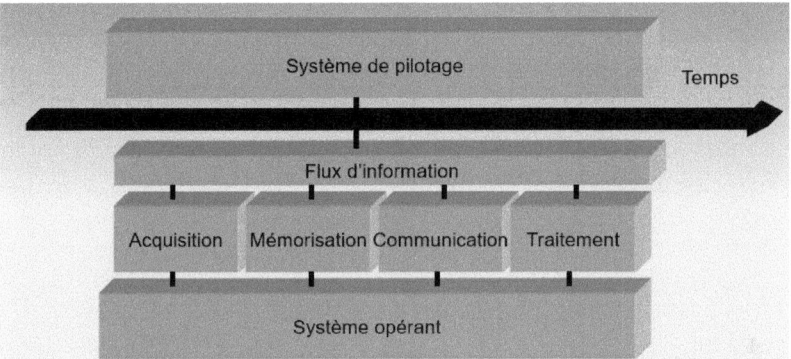

The operating system encompasses all actual production functions, such as processes and users. Today, a significant portion of the information flow is computerized, implying that computer security is increasingly synonymous with information system security and confidentiality.

In the field of computer security, the human factor plays a crucial role. Human errors can compromise the security of both the system and information, underscoring the importance of raising awareness and training users in security best practices.

The concept of computer security also entails a trade-off between cost, power, and time. For instance, the more information needs to be secure and confidential over an extended period, the higher the associated costs will be. Similarly, maintaining a system's availability 24/7 with minimal downtime requires significant investments. Hence, it is crucial to strike a balance between different security attributes (integrity, availability, confidentiality) based on financial and temporal constraints.

The impact of time on computer security must also be considered. The concepts of sustainability, availability, and integrity are linked to the duration for which these attributes need to be upheld. It is necessary to quantify what is acceptable or unacceptable for the company, administration, or project, considering temporal constraints.

The four attributes of the information flow (acquisition, storage, communication, processing) should be viewed through the lens of sustainability, availability, and integrity. Each attribute raises questions such as the acceptable loss of information, system downtime duration, the volume of corrupted information, etc.

In summary, computer security is a complex field that requires a holistic approach, considering the information flow, the operating system, the human factor, and security attributes. By evaluating costs, power, and time, it is possible to implement appropriate security measures to protect information and ensure the system's proper functioning.

CHAPTER 1.2: TIME, MEASUREMENT, EVALUATION, AND CONFIDENTIALITY

"Quality time is a precious jewel; at every moment it shines and nourishes the spirit."

It is important to determine the duration during which an element of the operating system can acquire, communicate, memorize, or process data, as well as the volume of data involved.

The Human Factor

Humans play an essential role in both the control system and the operating system. They are considered a distinct subsystem of the information system, with their own reality.

Theories of organization and the systemic approach often originated in the military-industrial complex before expanding into the public sector and then reaching the secondary and tertiary sectors, evolving with the field of socio-economics.

One of the proponents of these theories in the private sector (secondary and tertiary) is H. J. LEAVITT, in the 1950s, with his famous diagram known as "Leavitt's diamond." This is characterized by the following axiom: every behavior is initiated by one or more causes, determined by one or more motives, and always directed toward a single goal.

In our context, we focus on the concept of "motive," limiting ourselves to Maslow's hierarchy of needs. As long as we are in the lower part of the pyramid, i.e., physiological needs, the resulting behaviours are relatively similar from one individual to another. However, once the "psychological" aspect comes into play, behaviours become very different from one individual to another and depend on factors such as time and environment (individual's history, duration of exposure, etc.).

It is essential to consider the environment outside the company's information system, as an individual belongs to multiple information systems (family, religious, sports club, neighbourhood, etc.). These external information systems can influence the behaviours and attitudes of individuals in the context of the company.

Considering the human factor in cybersecurity is crucial. behaviours, motivations, and needs of individuals can impact how information is processed, communicated, and utilized. Therefore, it is essential to raise awareness among users about good security practices and implement control and monitoring mechanisms to prevent human errors and malicious behaviours.

In summary, the human factor is a key element to consider in managing cybersecurity. Understanding the behaviours, motivations, and needs of individuals can help design appropriate security measures, promote a security culture, and minimize risks associated with human errors.

CHAPTER 1.3: THE HUMAN GENERATOR OF AMBIGUITY

"In the face of the universe's chaos, the wise human gracefully dances in harmony with the forces of destiny."

According to the theories of JC MARCH and JP OLSEN in their famous 1972 "Garbage Can Theory of Organization," concerning the concept of organizational vagueness, we can identify four types of fuzzy behaviours partly related to the human system problem: objectivity, subjectivity, factual, and emotional.

There are different, even divergent, logics between humans and computers. The human factor is characterized by an uneven distribution, among individuals, between the objective and the subjective, as well as between the factual and the emotional. In contrast, computer logic is more focused on an objective and factual mode of operation, with less dominant influence from subjective and emotional factors, at least for now. These differences in logic and operation can lead to potential conflicts, requiring adaptation of systems and procedures to reconcile these differences and avoid malfunctions.

Here are some examples of malfunctions related to human logic:

Understanding Vagueness: Occurs when the environment is not clearly defined, and training to handle the four attributes of the information system is incomplete or non-existent.

Intention Vagueness: arises when the goals of the information system are poorly defined. Often, a lack of understanding leads to intention vagueness.

Historical Vagueness: Manifests when an event unexpectedly occurs in the information system. Thus, a lack of understanding and/or intention can lead to historical vagueness.

Organizational Vagueness: Occurs whenever the steering system modifies the rules of the operating system. During this period encompassing the beginning and end of the modification, there is organizational vagueness, which can be very localized and short-lived.

Understanding these concepts of organizational vagueness is essential for better grasping the interactions between the human factor and information systems. By understanding and managing these differences, it is possible to minimize potential conflicts and ensure harmonious operation between humans and computers.

At the operating level of a steering system, vague and imprecise information and directives can pose risks to information security. Here are some reasons why this can be problematic:

Misunderstanding Expectations: when information and directives are vague, it can be challenging for operators to clearly understand what is expected of them in terms of information security. This can lead to misinterpretations, inappropriate actions, or the improper implementation of security measures.

Incorrect Decision-Making: when provided information is imprecise, operators may make decisions based on assumptions or hypotheses, leading to errors in judgment. For example, they might overlook essential security measures or adopt risky behaviours, thinking they are acting in accordance with the guidelines.

Inconsistency in Security Practices: The absence of precise directives can lead to inconsistent security practices within the organization. Each operator may adopt different approaches or interpret instructions in their own way, creating vulnerabilities and inconsistencies in the implementation of security measures.

Difficulty in Evaluating Performance: when directives are unclear, it becomes challenging to objectively assess the compliance and effectiveness of implemented security measures. Without clear criteria, it is complicated to measure performance, identify gaps, and make improvements.

Lack of Accountability: when information and directives are unclear, it can be difficult to determine who is responsible for their implementation and follow-up. This can lead to a lack of accountability, compromising the overall effectiveness of information security.

To mitigate these risks, it is essential to provide clear and precise information and directives at the operational level. This can be achieved by developing detailed security policies, standardized operational procedures, specific instructions, and providing adequate training to operators. Effective and transparent communication is also crucial to clarify expectations and address any potential questions from operators.

In summary, vague and imprecise information and directives at the operational level pose risks to information security due to poor understanding, incorrect decision-making, inconsistent practices, difficulty in evaluating performance, and lack of accountability. A clear and precise approach is necessary to ensure the effective implementation of security measures and reduce the impacts of potential risks.

CHAPTER 1.4: THREATS, RISKS, AND ERRORS

"The wise one understands that the greatest risk is not taking any risk at all."

Error, inherent to human activity, is often seen as a weakness. However, according to Paul Claudel in his 1930 journal, "error is the cause of progress," suggesting that mistakes can be sources of learning and development. In a way, creativity can only emerge when we take risks and venture off the beaten path.

In the context of information systems, A.D. Swain and H.E. Guttman identified five types of errors that can occur:

Omission Error: this occurs when a planned procedure is not executed in the information system. For example, an employee may forget to enter certain information into software.

Execution Error: here, the execution differs from what was initially planned. For example, a user may select the wrong option in a drop-down menu.

Drift Error: This error occurs when unforeseen executions are introduced into the information system. For example, unauthorized changes may be made to the database.

Sequence Error: it occurs when actions are performed in a temporal order different from the one intended. For example, a series of tasks may be done in the wrong order.

Timing Error: this error concerns execution outside the prescribed deadlines. For example, an action may be performed too early or too late.

These errors can be classified into two main categories:

Failure Class: it encompasses errors related to system failures or organizational issues. For example, a computer system might crash due to a programming error.

Voluntary Class: this involves errors resulting from intentional human behaviours, usually related to individual needs satisfaction. For example, an employee may bypass security procedures to save time.

Understanding these errors is essential for assessing the risks to which an information system is exposed. Risk is a combination of the probability that a threat exploiting a specific vulnerability will occur and the impact it would have on the system. By identifying potential errors and the human factors contributing to them, system designers and managers can take measures to prevent or mitigate them.

In summary, error is an unavoidable reality, but it can be a driver of progress and innovation. Understanding the types of errors and the human behaviours underlying them is crucial for effectively managing risks in information systems and improving their reliability and security.

Risk assessment in an information system is a crucial step to ensure its security. In the context of data acquisition, it is essential to consider security attributes such as sustainability, availability, integrity, and the confidentiality attribute related to access authorization.

When discussing the sustainability of acquired data, we refer to the information system's ability to maintain the availability and integrity of data over the long term. Failure risks, such as hardware malfunctions or disasters, can compromise data sustainability and lead to loss or alteration. Therefore, it is crucial to assess the probability of these failures and their potential impact on acquired data.

The availability of resources necessary for acquisition is also an important aspect to consider. Failure risks, such as network or server breakdowns, can result in a halt in data acquisition. It is essential to assess the probability of these failures and implement backup and redundancy measures to ensure the continuous availability of resources.

Data integrity of acquired information is another critical aspect. Failure risks or transmission errors can alter the integrity of data and compromise their reliability. It is important to assess the risks associated with these failures and establish verification and validation mechanisms to prevent any undesirable alteration of acquired data.

Concerning confidentiality, the authorization attribute plays a key role. Intentional risks, such as sabotage, espionage, or fraud, can compromise the confidentiality of acquired data by allowing unauthorized access. It is essential to assess the risks of these threats and implement appropriate access controls, such as authentication and encryption measures, to ensure the confidentiality of acquired data.

Risk assessment in the context of data acquisition requires a thorough analysis of each security and confidentiality attribute, as well as various types of associated errors (omission, execution, drift, sequence, delay). This assessment helps identify potential risk impacts, estimate their probability of occurrence and impact, and implement appropriate security measures to mitigate these risks.

In conclusion, by understanding the risks associated with data acquisition in an information system, it is possible to take preventive measures to ensure the security and confidentiality of acquired data. Regular risk assessment and continuous monitoring are essential to maintain a safe and reliable computing environment.

In the realm of human behavior, there is a close connection between risk and delinquency. In this section, we will explore some avenues of thought to understand the transition from risk-taking to delinquency.

V.1 Behaviour and Risk

To incorporate the concepts of threat and vulnerability into human behaviour and define risky behaviour, it is essential to revisit the previously mentioned definition of risk. In this perspective, we will narrow down the notion of threat to aspects related to the limitation and satisfaction of psychological needs according to Maslow's hierarchy. Thus, we will consider threats that impact the satisfaction of these needs.

Threats can be classified based on different levels of Maslow's needs:

Security:

Challenge to an individual's position in society (e.g., threat of job loss).

Belongingness:

Rejection from a group or family, threat of exclusion.

Self-Esteem:

Threat of failure, illness, etc.

Esteem of Others:

Need for social recognition, betrayal by the group.

V.1.2 Vulnerability

Human vulnerability in an information system is largely linked to organizational ambiguity, which encompasses the three other types of ambiguity (technical, semantic, and cognitive). Vulnerability can make an individual more prone to taking risks and engaging in risky behaviours.

V.1.3 Risky Behaviour

The table below illustrates a correlation between different Maslow's needs and the types of errors associated with risky behaviour:

Maslow's Needs	Associated Risky Behaviours and Errors
Security	Engaging in behaviour that jeopardizes job security.
Belongingness	Participating in risky activities for group acceptance.
Self-Esteem	Taking excessive risks due to fear of failure.
Esteem of Others	Engaging in risky behaviour seeking social recognition or approval.

Aspect	Security	Belonging	Self-Esteem
Understanding	Drift, Omission	Execution, Delay	Omission, Delay
Intention	Drift, Omission	Delay, Sequence, Omission	Delay, Omission
Historical	Drift, Omission	Delay, Execution, Omission	Delay, Omission

V.2 Behaviour and Choices

In the face of risky behaviour, an individual has several possible choices. Risky behaviour can become a strategy to resolve a crisis situation generated by an aspect of organizational fuzziness. For example, due to a reorganization leading to a temporary lack of workforce, an employee may take the risk of bypassing certain control procedures to meet deadlines (voluntary omission error). This choice will heavily depend on their level of satisfaction of Maslow's needs.

It is also important to note that risky behaviors can be intentional or unintentional. Some individuals may be tempted to take risks for fun or out of boredom, while others may take risks with the intention of causing harm.

V.3 Behaviour and Delinquency

Delinquent behaviour in the field of cybersecurity is risky behaviour with the objective of causing harm. We can categorize cyber damages into two classes:

Sabotage: Intentional destruction, alteration, or subversion of systems, software, or information.

Espionage: Theft of confidential information, stealing hardware, or disclosing internal information.

Cyber delinquency can be motivated by various factors such as opportunity (a failure of the failure class may open the door to intentional error), revenge, fraud, or competition (e.g., industrial espionage or hacking activities).

It is essential to emphasize that cyber delinquency is primarily an organizational and human problem, less related to technical factors. According to some studies, approximately 80% of damages are caused by individuals internal to the organization. Common types of cybercrimes include embezzlement, information theft, program alteration, hardware destruction, unauthorized use of services, fraudulent data modification, and software theft.

In conclusion, understanding the relationship between human behaviour, risk, and delinquency is crucial to ad-dress cybersecurity issues comprehensively. By focusing on psychological needs, vulnerabilities, and the choices underlying these behaviours, it is possible to better understand the motivations and factors contributing to delinquency in the context of cybersecurity.

According to T.C. Richard (1986), unfortunately still relevant (Gardner Group), the Pareto principle holds true: 80% of the damages are caused by insiders.

The distribution by offenses is as follows:

1. Embezzlement: 34.1%
2. Information Theft: 13.6%
3. Program Alteration: 13.1%
4. Hardware Destruction: 11.3%
5. Unauthorized Use of Services: 9.6%
6. Fraudulent Data Modification: 7.1%
7. Software Theft: 6.5%

CHAPTER 1.5: STEERING SAFETY WITH HUMAN FACTORS

"The security is a journey, not a destination."

Having an appropriate methodology is essential for effectively addressing cybersecurity issues that incorporate human factors. The methodology I am most familiar with is the one I have designed and commercialized. However, there are other methodologies that may also be suitable. Once the basic principles are assimilated through a given methodology, it is then easy to create one's own methodology or use another.

It is important to emphasize that cybersecurity is not limited to the implementation of technical measures alone, but it also involves considering the behaviours and actions of individuals within an information system. Human factors play a crucial role in security because human errors, careless behaviours, and malicious actions can compromise the security of systems.

An effective methodology must, therefore, integrate awareness, training, and accountability measures for users. This may include security awareness campaigns, regular training on security best practices, the establishment of clear policies and procedures, as well as mechanisms for monitoring and evaluating user behaviours.

Furthermore, the methodology should also consider the psychological dimension of individuals. Understanding the motivations, perceptions, and behaviours of users regarding security is important. This allows adapting security measures according to the needs and specificities of each individual while fostering a security culture within the organization.

In summary, a suitable methodology for addressing cybersecurity issues that incorporate human factors is essential to ensure the protection of systems. It must consider technical, behavioural, and psychological aspects and include measures for user awareness, training, and accountability. By using an appropriate methodology, organizations can better understand and manage risks related to human factors, thereby contributing to strengthening the security of their information systems.

The methodology according to platforms like AITEK offers a performance and risk management approach aimed at providing business professionals with the means to make informed decisions and steering, particularly in security management that integrates human factors. It is based on a methodological shift from Business Intelligence to Business Investigation (BI++: according to AITEK platforms 1 and

GPS: according to AITEK platforms 2 and 3), aiming to better meet the needs of decision-makers.

One of the main issues that the methodology according to AITEK platforms seeks to address is the large number of irrelevant indicators generated by existing applications. On average, only 40% of these indicators are truly relevant and meet the needs of decision-makers. This is due to poorly expressed, transcribed, or interpreted objectives, as well as uncertainties about interpretation, information reliability, links with organizational objectives, and possibilities for action.

The methodology according to AITEK platforms aims to reduce this "loss" by tracking the causes of this inefficiency. It provides a methodological template to decision-makers, helping them answer the following questions:

What are the facts and reality my company is facing?

What are my objectives, and where do I want to take my company?

Which performance indicators should be measured to assess performance?

Which qualitative indicators should be considered, finally integrating the human factor?

By integrating these elements, the methodology according to AITEK platforms allows for more precise management of performance and risks, providing relevant indicators adap-ted to the organization's specific situation. It aims to empower business professionals with the decision-making tools necessary to effectively steer their businesses.

Indeed, in the Aitek methodology, performance is defined as achieving the desired results in each activity, seeking to obtain the right things, in the best way, and at optimal cost. This means that performance is assessed along three dimen-sions: results, process efficiency/know-how, and cost control/means.

In this approach, performance indicators are classified in a three-dimensional manner for each activity. This allows for evaluating performance according to these three criteria and determining appropriate measures for each aspect.

Moreover, it is important to note that each activity is linked to a requirement of the overall organization's objective. Each objective systematically involves a major associated risk. Thus, in the Aitek methodology, risk management is integrated into performance management. It is crucial to consider these risks when evaluating performance and implement measures to mitigate or control them.

In summary, the methodology according to AITEK platforms adopts a three-dimensional approach to performance, eva-luating results, process, and costs. It also integrates risk management by identifying major risks associated with each objective and taking measures to manage them effec-tively. This allows organizations to optimize their steering by aligning activities with objectives, measuring perfor-mance appropriately, and managing risks proactively.

In the Aitek methodology, the goal is to create a strong link between IT security, human factors, and the entire organization. This means that IT security and concerns related to human resources must be integrated in a cross-cutting manner and aligned with the overall business strategy.

For this purpose, each business unit and each profession must embody the organization's mission and translate this mission into specific requirements and risks that are unique to them. These requirements and risks are defined based on the organization's overall objectives and the specific characteristics of each industry. They serve as the foundation for developing action programs specific to each entity.

Each program is designed within its own context, taking into account the mission requirements, business specifics, and associated risks. This allows for defining clear and measurable objectives for each program.

Once the objectives are defined, it is essential to determine the activities necessary to achieve them. These activities may include information security measures, training to enhance employees' skills, continuous improvement processes, awareness campaigns, etc. Measures and indicators are then defined based on three key dimensions: expected results (impact), necessary know-how, and required resources (means).

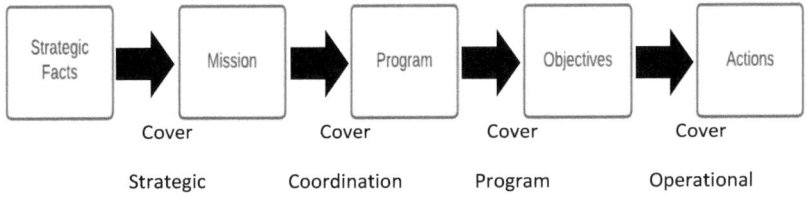

Figure 1 Facts Coordination

The three-dimensional classification of indicators allows for assessing performance in a holistic manner, considering the achieved results, mobilized skills, and invested resources. This approach promotes an integrated view of performance, emphasizing effectiveness, efficiency, and resource optimization.

By adopting this methodology, organizations can better align their information security and human factors with their strategic objectives. Each business unit and each profession are empowered in the implementation of the mission and corresponding action programs. This ensures consistent risk management, performance optimization, and a culture of security and shared responsibility at all levels of the organization.

In the Aitek methodology, each measure is structured by business entity, allowing for the definition of specific performance metrics for each area of activity. This structuring can include categories, types, geographical zones, age classes, etc. In parallel, an analysis entity is defined to enable a detailed identification of measures, whether it's by employee number, router number, or any other relevant pa-rameter.

Each measure is assigned a value between 0 and 1, which is then converted into a percentage based on a specific percentile related to the analysis of past data or manual calibration. This approach allows the aggregation of qualitative information (no, yes weakly, yes moderately, yes strongly) by associating percentiles with corresponding values. Thus, with only 10 or 100,000 $, it is possible to aggregate percentiles.

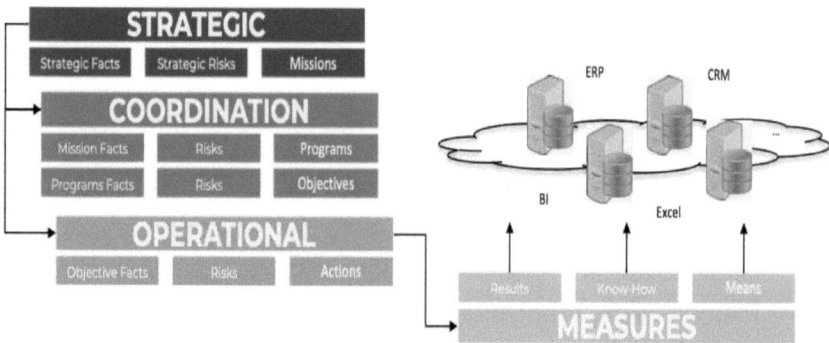

Subsequently, the weighted aggregation of percentiles for outcome measures determines the performance of the achieved results. The same process applies to skills and resources, following the Aitek methodology. These aggregations enable the generation of a three-dimensional performance assessment of objectives for each business unit.

Range	Qualification
0% - 45%	Low
46% - 60%	Correct
61% - 100%	Good

By employing a performance hierarchy structure, it becomes feasible to deduce the performance of programs, business units, and missions by aggregating the performances of corresponding activities. This approach facilitates a comprehensive and cohesive assessment of performance at all levels of the organization, ensuring strategic alignment and a holistic view of performance management.

Measure		
Business unit (sales representative)	Frequency (month)	Measure (TO)
Salesman 1	Jan-07	50 000
Salesman 2	Jan-07	20 000

Performance			
Nul (0%)	Small (33%)	Medium (66%)	High (100%)
0	10 000	10 001	20 000	20 001	65 000	65 001	99 999
0	1 000	1 001	5 000	5 001	15 000	15 001	25 000

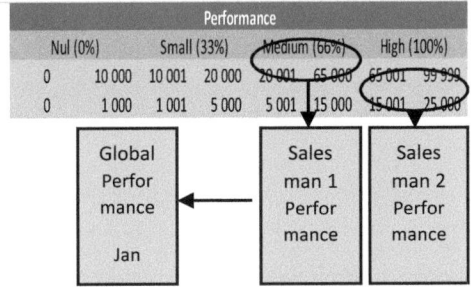

In summary, the methodology according to AITEK-type platforms enables the precise and entity-specific structuring and evaluation of performance, particularly in the context of IT security issues integrating human factors. The weighted aggregation of measures and percentiles allows for determining the three-dimensional performance of objectives, programs, business units, and missions, providing a comprehensive and aligned view of organizational performance.

CHAPTER 1.6: ANTICIPATION AND ACTION PLAN

"Anticipation is the key to peace of mind."

Even though risk levels may be similar, environments can vary significantly. In the desert, there might be no civilization within a 500 km radius, but over time, the landscape changes. Oil may be discovered nearby, and a road might pass by a house. Vulnerability remains the same, but the presence of new threats increases the overall risk.

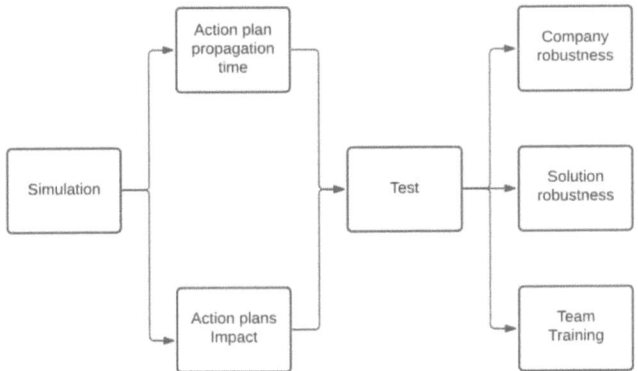

The risk management methodology of a platform like AITEK also emphasizes causation-correlation. The intelligent machine learning system has a conscious understanding of the stimuli it receives. It establishes connections between different pieces of information, investigates causes, and identifies correlations. This allows AITEK-type platforms to process situations, generate alarms, and propose optimal action plans.

To facilitate this process, organizations need to format their data and processes according to the concepts and notions of AITEK-type platforms. This involves strategic alignment, linking objectives, requirements, risks, and actions, and using composite measures of activities based on results, know-how, and means. This interconnection is achieved through a structured tree-shaped model that represents cause-and-effect relationships.

In essence, utilizing advanced risk management techniques by AITEK-type platforms enables businesses to proactively address threats, eliminate vulnerabilities, and optimize their performance. By understanding the subtleties of risk factors and leveraging causality relationships, AITEK-type platforms enable organizations to make informed decisions and effectively mitigate potential damages.

The solution of a platform like AITEK leverages the power of machine learning to analyze and process data, providing diagnostic capabilities that generate reports, dashboards, and alarms. The information obtained through machine learning algorithms provides valuable insights for informed decision-making and facilitates the implementation of effective action plans.

Once the data is analyzed by machine learning models, the solution generates comprehensive reports. These reports capture key findings, trends, and patterns discovered through analysis, presenting them in a structured and easily understandable format. Reports offer valuable insights into the underlying data, providing stakeholders with an overall view of the analyzed information.

In addition to reports, the AITEK-type platform solution creates dynamic dashboards that display real-time or near-real-time data visualizations. These dashboards serve as interactive interfaces, providing users with a customizable view of the analyzed data. Users can easily explore and interact with different visualizations, such as charts and tables, to gain deeper insights and monitor key performance indicators.

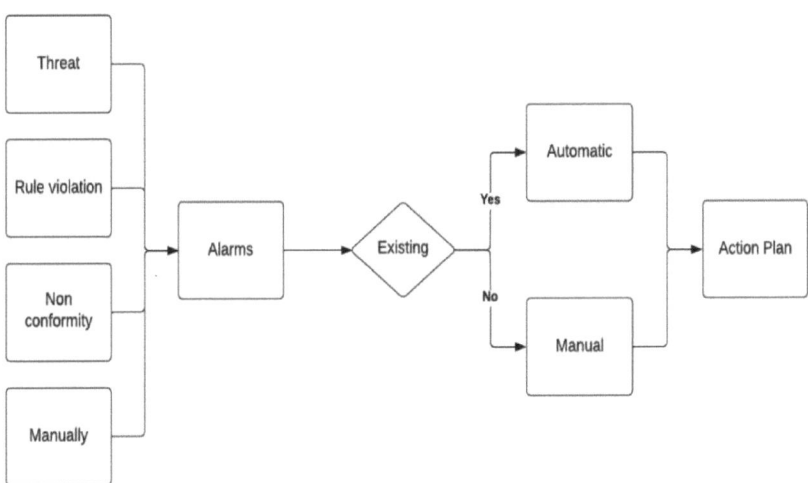

Furthermore, the solution incorporates an alarm system that detects anomalies, deviations, or predefined thresholds in the data. When an alarm is triggered, it alerts the relevant stakeholders, enabling swift action to address critical situations or opportunities. Alarms can be configured to notify specific individuals or teams, ensuring that the right people are informed promptly and can initiate appropriate action plans based on the information provided by machine learning models.

The generated reports, dynamic dashboards, and alarm notifications serve as catalysts for action plans. Based on diagnostic findings and identified areas for improvement or concern, stakeholders can develop strategic initiatives, operational changes, or targeted interventions. These action plans are designed to optimize performance, mitigate risks, capitalize on opportunities, and generate positive outcomes based on insights derived from machine learning analysis.

By seamlessly integrating diagnostics with reports, dashboards, and alarms, the AITEK-type platform solution enables organizations to make data-driven decisions, effectively monitor performance, and take proactive measures to achieve their objectives. The seamless integration of machine learning analysis with actionable results allows for continuous improvement and promotes successful outcomes across various fields and industries.

Threats, Alarms, and Action Plans

After the collection of on-site and external data, the crucial task of processing falls to Intelligent Agents, which are specialized algorithms and systems. Their primary goal is to comprehensively analyze the collected data, enabling them to identify potential threats, trigger alarms, and initiate appropriate action plans.

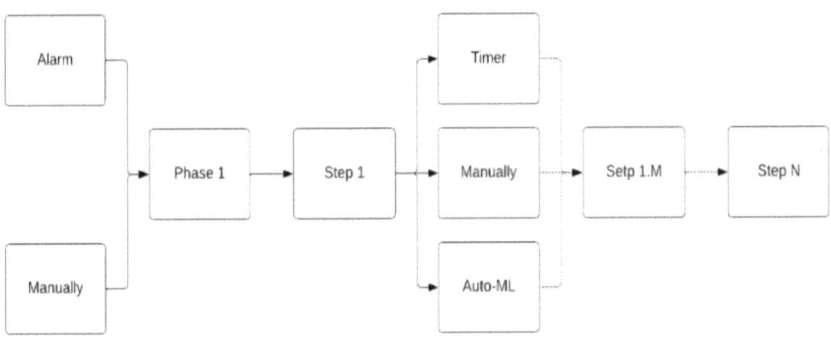

The Intelligent Agents utilize advanced techniques such as machine learning and data analysis to extract valuable information from the collected data. Through pattern recognition, anomaly detection, and predictive modeling, they can identify patterns, trends, and correlations that may indicate the presence of threats or risks within the dataset.

When a threat or risk is identified, Intelligent Agents quickly trigger alarms or notifications to alert the relevant stake-holders. These alarms can be transmitted through various channels to ensure that necessary personnel are promptly informed. The purpose of these alarms is to provide early warnings, enabling proactive measures to be taken before the situation escalates.

In addition to alarms, Intelligent Agents play a crucial role in initiating action plans. They leverage their analytical capabilities to generate recommendations or initiate prede-fined workflows aimed at effectively addressing identified threats or mitigating risks. These action plans may involve implementing security measures, notifying key personnel, executing contingency strategies, or adapting operational procedures as needed.

The strength of Intelligent Agents lies in their ability to rapidly and accurately process vast volumes of data. They continuously learn and adapt to new information, thereby enhancing their capabilities for threat detection and response over time. This adaptive nature allows them to stay ahead of emerging risks and evolving threats.

By harnessing the power of Intelligent Agents, orga-nizations can proactively detect and manage threats, strengthen their security measures, and ensure the continuity of their operations. Integrating these agents into the data processing flow enables businesses to make quick and informed decisions, protect their assets, and minimize potential damages.

Alarms

• Automatic Identification by Artificial Intelligence: the solution uses advanced artificial intelligence algorithms to automatically identify and recognize patterns indicative of potential threats. By leveraging machine learning and data analysis techniques, the system can detect abnormal behaviors or indicators signaling an increased risk.

• Manual Input during Model Building: Additionally, users have the option to manually input specific threats during the model-building process. This allows for the incorporation of domain-specific knowledge and expertise, ensuring comprehensive coverage of potential threats that may not be easily detectable solely through automated means.

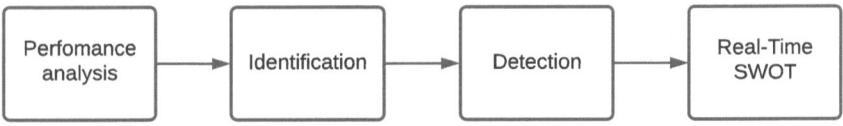

When a threat is detected, the system triggers two types of alarms to prompt appropriate actions:

Preventive Alarms: these alarms are designed to proactively inform users of an identified threat before it manifests as a significant risk. By alerting users in advance, preventive alarms enable them to take necessary measures, such as implementing security protocols, strengthening defenses, or initiating mitigation actions, to avoid potential risks' impacts and minimize their effects.

Corrective Alarms: corrective alarms are triggered when a threat has already materialized or poses an imminent danger. These alarms serve to inform users of the active presence of a threat, prompting immediate actions to address the situation, mitigate damages, and restore system security and stability.

By combining automated threat detection with manual inputs, the AITEK-type platform solution offers a comprehensive approach to identify and address potential threats. Preventive and corrective alarms allow for quick and appropriate responses, empowering users to proactively manage risks and safeguard their systems, data, and operations.

The AITEK-type platform solution provides a comprehensive alarm system that keeps users informed about various critical aspects of their operations. Alarms serve as notifications for the following scenarios:

Threats: when the system detects a potential threat or an external factor that could pose a risk to the business, an alarm is triggered. These threats can come from various sources and may include cybersecurity threats, operational risks, market volatility, or any other factor that could impact the organization's security or stability.

Rule Violations: a rule is a predefined and structured statement that defines constraints and controls in business processes. Violating these rules can have significant implications for the organization. The system monitors compliance with these rules and triggers an alarm in case of a violation. This contributes to ensuring compliance with regulatory requirements, internal policies, or industry standards.

Procedure Non-Compliance: procedures provide guidance on how to perform specific tasks or actions in the system. They define steps, protocols, and best practices to follow in various circumstances. In case of deviation from these procedures, indicating non-compliance, an alarm is gene-rated to alert the user. This helps maintain consistency, accuracy, and efficiency in the organization's operations.

When a supervisor encounters a new type of threat or alarm, they have the option to create and define it in the system. The supervisor associates the new alarm with an appropriate action plan, specifying the necessary steps to take in response to the alarm. As the system learns from these user-defined associations, it becomes capable of automatically assigning triggers to alarms and their corresponding action plans in the future. This automation streamlines the process and ensures a prompt and con-sistent response to emerging threats or critical situations.

Additionally, the AITEK-type platform solution includes a predictive component that enables preventive alarms. By analyzing significant changes in monitored variables, the system can anticipate potential issues or impacts of risks. It generates predictions at specific time intervals, such as T+1 week or T+1 month, and calculates associated perfor-mances and risks. Through simulations and future analyses, the system determines if these elements could trigger new alarms. If a future alarm is predicted, the corresponding action plan is automatically launched, allowing users to anticipate and proactively address potential risk impacts.

In summary, the alarm system of the AITEK-type platform solution keeps users informed about threats, rule violations, and procedure non-compliance. It allows users to create new alarms and associate them with action plans, while the system continuously learns and automates alarm assignments based on historical data. Moreover, the system's predictive capabilities facilitate preventive alarms, enabling proactive decision-making and risk management.

Action plans play a crucial role in the AITEK-type platform solution, representing the final step in the process. They consist of a series of predefined phases, composed of steps determined in collaboration with the client during the implementation phase.

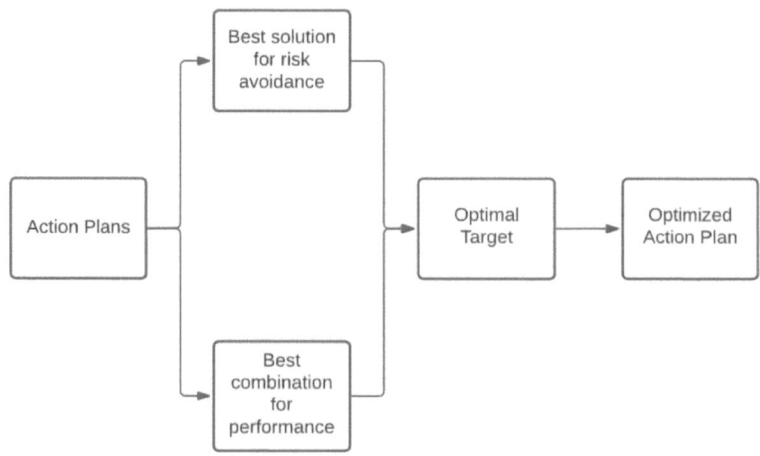

The activation of an action plan can occur either through the triggering of an alarm or manually initiated by the user. Progression from one phase to another is achieved by completing the individual steps described in each phase. These steps can be completed in one of the following ways:

Timer: the completion of a step can be time-based, where a specific duration is allocated for its execution. Once the timer elapses, the step is considered complete, and the action plan moves to the next phase.

Manual Intervention: a user or responsible person manually marks a step as completed, indicating that the necessary actions or tasks associated with that step have been accomplished.

Machine Learning (ML) Program: in some cases, the completion of a step can be automated through the execution of a Machine Learning (ML) program. This program performs the tasks and actions required for the step, enabling efficient and accurate progression in the action plan.

In the AITEK-type platform solution, there are two main types of action plans:

Strategic Action Plans: these plans are manually initiated and are associated with risks related to missions, objectives, or programs. They are designed to address challenges at the strategic level and ensure alignment of actions with organizational goals.

Operational Action Plans: these plans are triggered by alarms, indicating the need for immediate action in response to specific events or conditions. Operational action plans focus on quickly resolving issues and operational-level risks.

Each action plan is assigned a defined period, specifying its start and end dates. Additionally, a responsible person or manager is tasked with overseeing the execution of the action plan. This manager can be a human, an IoT device, or an intelligent agent, depending on the nature of the action plan and the tasks involved.

This approach to action plans brings significant value to the overall process. It allows for the evaluation and opti-mization of action plans over time, leading to continuous improvement and enhanced performance. Assigning a manager to each action plan facilitates performance com-parisons among the involved resources, enabling effective resource management and allocation.

In summary, the action plan in the AITEK-type platform solution is an essential component marking the final step of the process. It consists of predefined phases and steps, which can be completed through timers, manual inter-vention, or Machine Learning (ML) programs. Strategic and operational action plans address different types of risks and challenges. Including a responsible person or manager for each action plan ensures accountability and allows for per-formance evaluation. This comprehensive approach en-hances the efficiency and effectiveness of the action plan-ning process in the AITEK-type platform solution.

CHAPTER 1.7: SECURITY AND HUMAN FACTORS

"The order arises from the inner harmony of man."

In the Aitek methodology, the primary objective is to minimize risk. Since it is practically impossible to act directly on the threat itself, the approach focuses on reducing the organization's vulnerability. To achieve this, several measures are implemented:

<u>Eliminate Ambiguities</u>: training and information are utilized to ensure a clear understanding of risks and security measures. Strict work procedures, such as adopting standards like ISO 9001 or ISO 9004-3 (Continuous Character System and Processes), are established to clarify intentions and activity history.

<u>Limit Failure Errors</u>: test and pre-production environments are established to identify and rectify errors before they propagate into the production environment. Rigorous validation procedures and controlled transitions between environments are implemented to minimize failure risks.

<u>Limit Deliberate Errors</u>: Continuous monitoring is maintained to detect intentional errors. Human vigilance is established to identify signs of suspicious behaviour and take appropriate measures to prevent incidents.

<u>Manage Realized Risks</u>: swift detection of errors, regardless of their nature, is essential to react promptly and minimize damages. This also involves financial protection against production losses and potential legal consequences resulting from incidents, as well as safeguarding the organization's reputation.

In light of this introduction, risk reduction means can be classified into four categories: prevention, detection, protection, and insurance.

Prevention involves taking proactive measures to reduce risk. This includes establishing clear procedures, employee awareness and training, and adopting standards and best practices to ensure compliance and minimize vulnerabilities.

In summary, the Aitek methodology emphasizes prevention by reducing vulnerability, quickly detecting errors, protecting against potential damages, and providing financial and legal assurance. These combined measures reduce risks and ensure a safe and secure operation of the organization.

After addressing prevention, the Aitek methodology moves to the protection phase. The goal is to reduce the effects of potential damage. Here are the key elements of this phase:

Validation and Environment: every new component (hardware, tool, procedure, pro-gram, version, etc.) must undergo unit and non-regression tests by the project team. These tests are conducted according to defined plans in a test environment, and deployment and modification procedures are documented. An independent project validation team is responsible for authorizing the transition to pre-production based on test results and procedure quality. Innovations are then deployed in a pre-production environment for integration and non-regression tests performed by a group of real users and pilots. Again, the validation team authorizes the transition to pre-production based on test results and procedure quality. The minimum required three environments are:

Test environment: Represents the production structure with lower data volumes.

Pre-production environment: Reflects the production environment (only alphanumeric data is encrypted when updating data and synchronized at a determined frequency).

Production environment: Represents the finished product. It is crucial to manage consistency between different versions extremely strictly to avoid, for example, an obsolete tool disrupting the information system. This precaution helps limit failure errors.

To limit hardware failure errors, it is recommended to apply methods used in the industry. Each hardware component has a theoretical lifespan (MTBF) specified by the manufacturer and usage conditions. Sensitive elements should be replaced at 90% of their lifespan, and during this maintenance operation, it is important to verify that usage conditions are correct.

Similarly, humans have a limit of interest in the tasks they perform. Therefore, it is necessary to plan job changes and training for new tasks before reaching this limit.

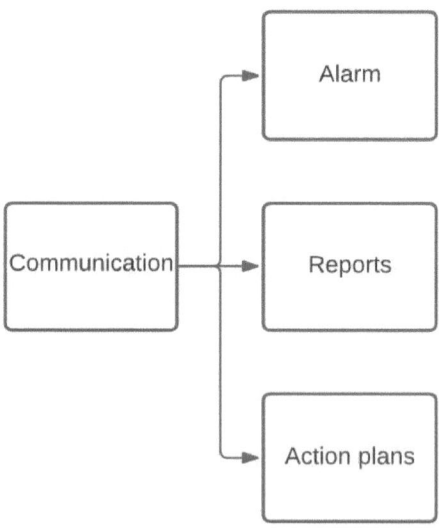

Other protection measures include strict control of incoming and outgoing flows (antivirus, limitation of access to sites based on roles, strict rules regarding email attachments, etc.) and the systematic use of uninterruptible power supplies, surge protectors, and firewalls.

Protection aims to reduce the effects of potential damage by implementing appropriate controls and security measures. The Aitek methodology addresses this phase after establishing robust prevention measures to ensure the security of information systems and human factors.

Backup, restoration, and recovery are essential elements in the Aitek methodology to ensure the protection of data and information systems. They aim to minimize data losses in case of hardware failure, software failure, natural disasters, or human incidents.

To establish an effective backup strategy, it is important to determine the elements to be backed up. This includes human, hardware, software, and paper aspects. On the human side, situations such as resignations, illnesses, vacations, or personal issues that could lead to partial or total absence of a person should be considered. For hardware, it is necessary to back up disks, central processing units, backup units, routers, network cards, and peripherals. Concerning software, the operating system, operational programs such as Word, Oracle, SAP, and data associated with these programs should be backed up. Finally, paper documents such as notices, documentation, and procedures should also be backed up, preferably by scanning them for better electronic document management (EDM).

To define an effective backup strategy, it is necessary to answer several key questions. Firstly, the acceptable level of information loss must be determined. Then, the time allowed for backup and the acceptable recovery time in case of disaster should be defined. These factors will help determine the frequency of backups and the backup methods to use.

It is important to formalize backup, restoration, testing, and return-to-production procedures. These procedures must be clear, well-documented, and regularly updated to ensure correct and effective execution. They should be accessible to all team members responsible for data backup and restoration.

In the implementation of the backup strategy, it is essential to consider the human factor. Replacement strategies should be planned for key personnel to ensure that backup and restoration operations can be performed even in case of absence or unexpected departure. It is recommended to assign the "backup" role to trained individuals and ensure adequate coordination to ensure smooth procedure execution.

For hardware, it is essential to have a minimum buffer stock to cope with hardware failures and strict agreements on guaranteed delivery and installation times for replacement hardware.

For software, there are different types of backups that can be used based on needs. Full backups involve backing up the entire system on an external or removable medium such as CD, hard drive. It is recommended to keep multiple sets of backups to avoid data loss in case of backup failure. Incremental backups only backup changes made since the last full or incremental backup. Backups can be performed hot, i.e., while the system is operational, or cold, when the system is shut down.

In the case of database management systems (DBMS) such as Oracle, SQL Server, DB2, there are logical and physical backups. Logical backups involve translating data into another format for backup, while physical backups involve a physical copy of the database files. Some architectures may also have data duplication mechanisms, such as standby or high-availability systems, which allow for a synchronized or even operational backup system in case of failure of the main system.

Concerning paper documents, it is recommended to scan information and integrate it into an electronic document management (EDM) system to facilitate storage, search, and retrieval. However, some information may require paper outputs, such as printing reports or consolidated data.

It is important to consider the longevity of backups, especially in sectors such as the medical or food industry. Technological advances can make certain backup media obsolete, making it difficult or even impossible to read them later. Therefore, it is essential to plan for regular migration and update methods for backups to ensure their long-term accessibility.

In summary, backup, restoration, and recovery of data and information systems are essential elements to ensure the protection of critical information. Adequate planning, clear procedures, and proper training of staff are indispensable to ensure data availability in case of disaster.

Detection is a crucial step in information security management, as it allows for the early identification of the transition from a potential risk to actual damage. To achieve this goal, it is essential to collect and analyze various traces left by actions in the information system.

Traces can take different forms and are crucial for spotting early signs of security issues. For example, virus signatures, cookies, temporary or work files, replication elements, and historical files are important indicators to consider. These traces allow for the detection of anomalies, suspicious behaviors, or malicious actions and enable timely response. Here are some key aspects of detection in the Aitek methodology:

VI.2.1 Log Monitoring:

Regular monitoring of system activity logs allows for the detection of unusual patterns or events. Logs may include information about connections, unauthorized access attempts, configuration changes, etc. The implementation of log management systems and automated analysis tools facilitates this monitoring.

VI.2.2 Network Traffic Analysis:

Analysis of network traffic helps detect suspicious behaviors, such as intrusion attempts or unauthorized communications. Intrusion detection systems and intrusion prevention systems are used to monitor network traffic in real-time.

VI.2.3 Behavioural Analysis:

Monitoring the behaviour of users and systems can reveal abnormal activities. This includes detecting sudden changes in usage patterns, repeated attempts of unauthorized access, or any activity deviating from normal patterns.

VI.2.4 Vulnerability Analysis:

Regular assessment of system vulnerabilities helps detect weaknesses that could be exploited by attackers. Automated vulnerability scans help identify security flaws and take corrective actions.

VI.2.5 Use of Intrusion Detection Systems (IDS):

IDS are tools specifically designed to detect suspicious or malicious activities. They analyze network traffic, system logs, and other sources to identify anomalies and trigger real-time alerts.

VI.2.6 Use of Malware DetectionSystems:

Malicious software, such as viruses and malware, can cause significant damage. Malware detection systems are used to identify the presence of malicious code on systems.

VI.2.7 Intrusion Testing:

Intrusion testing, also known as penetration testing, involves simulating attacks on the system to assess its resistance to threats. These tests help identify potential weaknesses and strengthen security.

Detection in the Aitek methodology relies on a combination of automated monitoring, data analysis, and the use of specialized tools to quickly identify potential threats. By detecting anomalies at an early stage, the organization can take measures to mitigate risks and protect its systems.

After detection, the Aitek methodology focuses on the assurance phase. The goal of this phase is to assess the effectiveness of implemented security measures, ensure compliance with standards and regulations, and guarantee appropriate risk management. Here are the main elements of the assurance phase:

VI.3.1 Security Audit:

Security audits involve evaluating all security measures in place. This includes reviewing security policies, operational procedures, system configurations, access permissions, etc. Audits can be conducted at regular intervals to ensure continuous compliance.

VI.3.2 Standards Compliance:

Ensuring compliance with relevant security standards for the industry is essential. This may include standards such as ISO 27001 for information security, PCI DSS for credit card payments, HIPAA for health information protection, etc.

VI.3.3 Risk Assessment:

Continuous risk assessment ensures that new potential threats are considered, and security measures are adjusted accordingly. This involves regular analysis of vulnerabilities, potential impacts, and probabilities of occurrence.

VI.3.4 Security Testing:

Security testing includes attack simulations, intrusion tests, and other methods to assess the system's resistance to threats. These tests help identify potential weaknesses and enhance security.

VI.3.5 Incident Management:

Incident management involves establishing clear procedures to respond to security breaches. This includes defining intervention plans, notifying stakeholders, collecting information about the incident, and post-incident analysis to strengthen security measures.

VI.3.6 Ongoing Training:

Ongoing staff training is essential to maintain a strong security culture within the organization. This includes awareness of new threats, the importance of compliance with security measures, and the proper response to security incidents.

The assurance phase in the Aitek methodology ensures a continuous and comprehensive evaluation of security measures, aiming to maintain a robust and effective security posture. It encompasses regular audits, compliance checks, risk assessments, testing, incident response planning, and ongoing training to adapt to evolving security challenges.

This concludes Chapter 1.7 on Security and Human Factors in the Aitek methodology. The emphasis on prevention, protection, detection, and assurance reflects a holistic approach to information security management, considering both technical and human aspects to create a resilient and secure organizational environment.

CHAPTER 1.8: HUMAN INTELLIGENCE - THE ART OF ANTICIPATION

"Look at the sky even before the rain starts to fall."

Human watch constitutes a fundamental aspect of overall security in the Aitek methodology. It relies on the art of anticipation, aiming to identify early signs of potential threats and take preventive measures. This chapter explores the importance of human watch in the context of cybersecurity.

I. Introduction to Human Watch:

Human watch encompasses the continuous monitoring of activities, behaviors, and trends that could pose potential risks to security. Unlike automated systems, human watch relies on intuition, experience, and the ability to interpret subtle signals.

II. Foundations of the Art of Anticipation:

Behavioural Analysis: Professionals in human watch develop a deep understanding of normal and abnormal behaviours. This includes observing employee interactions, detecting sudden behaviour changes, and recognizing unusual patterns.

Discreet Monitoring: The art of anticipation often relies on discreet monitoring. This can include supervision of physical and electronic access, monitoring communications, and detecting weak signals that might indicate an imminent threat.

III. Human Watch and Human Factors:

Training and Awareness: Employees are key players in human watch. Their training and awareness of risks contribute to strengthening the first line of defense. Recognizing social engineering tactics and empowering employees in security are crucial aspects.

Internal Communication: Effective communication within the organization facilitates the sharing of information about potential threats. Clear and confidential communication channels are established to encourage reporting of suspicious activities.

IV. Emotional Intelligence in Human Watch:

Understanding Motivations: The ability to understand human motivations is essential. Professionals in human watch must anticipate potential actions by understanding motivations, frustrations, and triggering factors.

Crisis Management: Emotional intelligence also plays a role in crisis management. The ability to stay calm, make informed decisions under pressure, and manage emotions within the team contributes to an effective response.

V. Collaboration and Partnerships:

Information Sharing: Human watch often extends beyond organizational boundaries. Partnerships and information-sharing networks enable collective watch, enhancing the ability to anticipate threats that could have a sector-wide impact.

Cooperation with Authorities: Collaboration with relevant authorities strengthens human watch on a broader level. Exchanging information with national security agencies contributes to a more comprehensive understanding of potential threats.

VI. Technology in Service of Human Watch:

Integration of AI and Analytics: Artificial intelligence and analytics technologies are integrated to support human watch. This includes using machine learning to detect complex patterns and predictive analysis to anticipate emerging trends.

Automation of Routine Tasks: By automating repetitive tasks, professionals in human watch can focus on more in-depth analysis. Automation frees up time for critical human evaluation.

VI.4 Insurance: Transfer of Responsibility and Financial Costs

When damage occurs in the realm of cybersecurity, it often entails significant financial costs. These costs may be associated with system restoration, operational losses, damage to the company's image, or the inability to meet contractual obligations or deadlines.

To manage these financial risks effectively, resorting to insurance is crucial. Insurance enables the transfer of responsibility in case of damage, thus relieving the company of the financial burdens that ensue. However, for insurers and legal professionals to perform their roles effectively, it is crucial to have accurate traces and information about the events leading to the damage.

This is why the collection and preservation of traces, as mentioned in Chapter VI.2 on detection, are of great importance. Traces, whether event logs, connection logs, or other types of information, allow retracing the steps that led to the damage and identifying the responsibilities of each party.

Simultaneously, it is essential to keep licenses and maintenance contracts up to date. These legal documents define the obligations and responsibilities of the involved parties, facilitating the insurance and financial risk management processes.

From an accounting perspective, it is recommended to allocate potential costs related to cybersecurity. This means creating a financial reserve to address unforeseen expenses in case of damage.

Finally, the importance of managing confidentiality and liability clauses in employment contracts should be emphasized. These clauses contribute to protecting sensitive company information and establishing employees' responsibilities regarding cybersecurity.

In summary, insurance plays a crucial role in managing financial risks related to cybersecurity. To optimize this process, it is necessary to have accurate traces, keep licenses and contracts up to date, allocate potential costs, and manage confidentiality and liability clauses in employment contracts.

VII. Men and Security: Role and Management

VII.1. Role within the Company: a Broad Spectrum of Expertise

The role of cybersecurity in companies, while not ancient, encompasses a significant spectrum of expertise. It includes technical skills such as test management, audits, control of standards, and diagnostic procedures. Additionally, it involves supervisory aspects like managing environments, backups, and traces. Furthermore, it requires collaboration with other departments, especially general security and human resources for training and human watch.

Hierarchically, it is incorrect to associate this function with the IT department. On the contrary, it should directly report to top management and have its own technical and relational team. Decoupling control and monitoring functions is crucial to avoid dependence that could impact mission results.

Regularly integrating external experts, despite higher costs, is also crucial. External experts bring neutrality compared to internal staff, ease in communicating messages (less subject to internal political pressures), up-to-date and sharp experience, as well as a fresh perspective on the company.

VII.2. Selection and Management of Internal and External Resources

VII.2.1 Recruitment: Assessing Cybercrime Risks

In recruitment criteria, it is essential to include the assessment of cybercrime risks. This considers security skills to prevent potential malicious actions.

VII.2.2 Monitoring: Training, Human Watch, and Employee Satisfaction

Regularly monitoring personnel in terms of training, human watch, and satisfaction is crucial. Team-building seminars and corporate events can be organized to strengthen team cohesion and motivation. The frequency of these activities should be adapted to the risk level in the area where personnel operate.

VII.2.3 Change Management

Change management and cybersecurity are interdependent aspects in the context of technological evolution and organizational transformations. When a company undergoes significant changes, such as adopting new technologies, migrating to the cloud, undergoing digital transformation, or implementing new processes, it is essential to consider cybersecurity risks that may arise during this transition period.

One major risk is the increased vulnerability of systems and data during change phases. When new infrastructures or applications are deployed, they may have undetected security flaws. Additionally, employees may be less familiar with new technologies or processes, leading to human errors and unintentional vulnerabilities.

Another risk is the elevated threat level during change periods. Cybercriminals often exploit transition times for attacks, as defenses may be weakened, or employees may be distracted by ongoing changes. Therefore, it is essential to intensify monitoring and detection of suspicious activities during change periods.

Employee awareness and training are also key elements of change management to mitigate cybersecurity risks. Employees must be informed about new security policies, best practices, and procedures to follow during transition periods. It is crucial to raise awareness about potential threats and educate them on secure behaviors.

Change management must also consider governance of cybersecurity. This involves ensuring that new change initiatives incorporate appropriate security measures from the outset. Security teams should be involved from the early stages of the change process to assess potential risks, recommend appropriate security measures, and ensure compliance with security standards and regulations.

Finally, communication and coordination between change management teams and cybersecurity teams are essential to ensure effective risk management during transition periods. Information exchange, collaboration, and shared accountability mechanisms help reduce security gaps and ensure a consistent and integrated approach to cyber-security.

In summary, change management and cybersecurity are closely linked. Considering security risks from the early stages of change planning, raising employee awareness and training, cybersecurity governance, and coordination bet-ween teams are essential measures to minimize vulnera-bilities and threats during transition periods. A proactive and integrated approach to change management and cy-bersecurity ensures operational continuity and protects the organization's assets and data.

Effective change management for human resources is a crucial aspect of modern organizational management. When a company undergoes significant changes such as the implementation of new technologies, the adoption of new processes, or restructuring, it is essential to proactively and effectively manage these changes to minimize resistance, maximize employee buy-in, and ensure the success of the transition.

Change management involves considering the human and organizational aspects of the change process. It aims to anticipate, understand, and manage reactions and impacts of changes on employees, ensuring they are well-prepared, supported, and involved throughout the process.

To effectively manage change at the human resources level, it is important to follow key steps. Firstly, clear and transparent communication about the reasons and objectives of the change is essential. Employees need to understand the necessity of the change and its impact on the organization and themselves. Open communication also fosters trust and employee engagement.

Next, it is crucial to involve employees in the change process actively. Their active participation allows for the collection of their ideas, concerns, and suggestions, promoting their engagement and strengthening their sense of belonging to the organization. Employee involvement can be facilitated through workgroups, brainstorming sessions, surveys, or consultation meetings.

Simultaneously, providing adequate training and support to employees is important to help them adapt to the changes. This may include training sessions on new skills or processes, reference resources, individual coaching, or mentoring programs. Continuous support throughout the change process enables employees to develop their skills and confidence, facilitating their transition to new ways of working.

Change management for human resources also requires proactive management of resistance to change. It is normal for some employees to express resistance or apprehension towards change. Therefore, it is essential to recognize these reactions and address them constructively. This may involve individual discussions, awareness sessions, clarification of expectations, or resolution of potential issues. The goal is to support employees in their adaptation process and help them overcome potential obstacles.

Finally, it is important to assess and measure the results of the change. Change management for human resources does not stop once the change is implemented. It is necessary to monitor and evaluate the impact of the change on employees, processes, and organizational outcomes. This allows for potential adjustments and identifies lessons learned for future changes.

VII.2.3 Contracts: Confidentiality and Liability Clauses

It is recommended to include confidentiality and liability clauses, with financial penalties for non-compliance with procedures, in all framework contracts with external service providers, as well as in employment contracts with internal employees. These clauses help reinforce individual responsibility and protect sensitive company information.

VII.2.4 Traces and Isolation of External Entities

For external service providers, implementing systematic traceability measures is essential. Traces should be integrated natively into the external role and stored appropriately. Moreover, it is advisable to confine external service providers to a subsystem in pseudo-isolation to limit their access to sensitive company resources.

In summary, the information security function should be positioned independently in the company, reporting directly to the top management. It is crucial to integrate external experts, consider risk assessment criteria during recruitment, ensure regular monitoring of personnel, and establish contracts with confidentiality and liability clauses. Traces must be collected systematically for both internal and external entities, and external service providers should be confined to a subsystem in pseudo-isolation.

VII.3 Legislation, Ethics, and Reality: legal Compliance and Ethical Considerations

Legal compliance and ethical considerations are crucial elements in the context of information security. Companies must not only adhere to data privacy and information protection laws and regulations but also adopt an ethical approach to guide their actions.

Legal compliance involves adhering to the specific laws and regulations of the country in which the company operates. This may include laws on personal data protection, copyrights, patents, and trademarks. Contracts with internal and external resources must include clauses detailing legal obligations and responsibilities regarding information security.

In parallel with legal compliance, ethical considerations must also be taken into account. Ethics involves moral principles, fairness, justice, and respect for human rights and dignity. Ethical conduct in the context of information security means acting responsibly, respecting data privacy, preventing abuses, and treating all concerned parties fairly.

Companies can develop a specific ethical charter that reflects their values and commitments to information security. This charter should define the ethical principles that all employees must adhere to, such as privacy respect, transparency, integrity, and responsibility.

However, it is important to note that the reality of human interactions can be complex and ambiguous. Decisions regarding information security may often face ethical dilem-mas, such as the tension between necessary surveillance to protect data and the respect for individuals' privacy. Companies must find a balance between the need to mitigate risks and respect the fundamental rights and freedoms of their employees and customers.

Therefore, it is essential to raise awareness among employees about ethical considerations and provide training on best practices in information security. This can be achieved through training programs, awareness sessions, and open discussions about the ethical dilemmas they may encounter in their work.

In summary, information security goes beyond legal compliance. Companies must also adopt an ethical approach to guide their actions concerning data security. This involves respecting laws and regulations but also acting responsibly, transparently, and respectfully toward all stakeholders. Employee awareness and training on ethical considerations are essential to promote a strong and ethical information security culture within the company.

CHAPTER 1.9: SOME EXAMPLES

"I hear and I forget, I see and I remember, I do and I understand."

Common Human-Engaged Cyber Attacks: Phishing and Social Engineering

1. Phishing Attack

Phishing is a prevalent method employed by cybercriminals to compromise the security of computer systems and pilfer sensitive information. This attack involves sending fraudulent electronic messages, such as emails or text messages, posing as legitimate entities like financial institutions, businesses, or government organizations. Cybercriminals utilize psychological manipulation techniques to coerce users into disclosing personal information like passwords, credit card numbers, or identification details.

Phishing emails are often crafted to appear legitimate, incorporating logos and layouts resembling those of targeted organizations. These messages may prompt recipients to click on malicious links redirecting them to fraudulent websites where their information is stolen or to download attachments infected with malware.

2. Social Engineering Attack

Social engineering is an attack technique that exploits psychological manipulation and individuals' trust to acquire confidential information or access protected systems. Cybercriminals employ tactics of persuasion and social engineering to manipulate individuals into divulging sensitive information or performing risky actions.

For instance, attackers may impersonate a company employee or legitimate IT technician, contacting an employee to request confidential information or gain access to protected systems. They might also pose as a colleague, friend, or family member to build trust with the victim and obtain sensitive information.

Social engineering attacks can manifest through phone calls, instant messages, in-person meetings, or even leveraging social media. Cybercriminals use psychological manipulation techniques, such as flattery, emotional manipulation, or authority manipulation, to deceive their victims.

In both phishing and social engineering attacks, the ultimate goal is to obtain sensitive information, such as login credentials, banking information, or personal data, for malicious purposes like identity theft, account hijacking, or financial fraud.

Protection Measures Against Phishing Attacks

To safeguard against phishing attacks, it is crucial to adopt best practices:

Clear Communication Policy:

Vigilance: be alert to unsolicited emails, messages, and phone calls requesting personal or financial information. Beware of urgent requests or threats of negative consequences if not responded to promptly.

Verify Authenticity: Before providing sensitive information, always verify the authenticity of the sender or caller. Use reliable sources for contact details rather than clicking on links or calling numbers provided in a suspicious email.

Protect Login Credentials: never share login credentials, passwords, or authentication codes with unauthorized third parties. Use strong, unique passwords for each account and enable two-factor authentication where possible.

Caution with Links and Attachments: avoid clicking on links or downloading attachments from unreliable or unknown sources. Check URLs before clicking and use antivirus software to detect malicious files.

Report Phishing Attempts: If you receive a suspicious email or communication, report it to your IT security team or service provider. This contributes to awareness and helps prevent future attacks.

Man-in-the-Middle (MITM) Attack

A Man-in-the-Middle (MITM) attack is a method of inter-cepting and manipulating communications between two parties seeking to communicate securely. In this type of attack, an adversary clandestinely inserts themselves bet-ween the two legitimate parties, intercepting all exchan-ged information.

The primary goal of the attacker in a MITM attack is to gain unauthorized access to sensitive data, such as login cre-dentials, financial information, or confidential messages. To achieve this, the attacker must be able to monitor and manipulate communications without being detected.

Various techniques can be employed to conduct a MITM attack. One common method involves impersonating the identity of a network access point or router. For instance, an attacker might create a malicious Wi-Fi network with a name similar to that of a legitimate network, enticing users to connect. Once connected, the attacker can intercept all network traffic and access sensitive data.

Another prevalent method is ARP (Address Resolution Protocol) cache poisoning, where the attacker alters IP-MAC correspondence tables on the local network. This enables the attacker to redirect legitimate network traffic to their own machine, where they can intercept and mani-pulate exchanged data.

A MITM attack can also be executed at the encrypted communication level, using decryption and re-encryption techniques. For example, the attacker might use a fraudulent certificate to impersonate a secure server, decrypting and accessing confidential data exchanged between legitimate parties.

The consequences of a MITM attack can be severe, allowing the attacker to gain unauthorized access to sensitive data, compromise communication confidentiality, and manipulate exchanged information. This can result in identity theft, financial fraud, data loss, and other detrimental outcomes for targeted individuals and organizations.

Protection Measures Against MITM Attacks

To safeguard against Man-in-the-Middle attacks, it is crucial to implement robust and enduring security measures. Here are some recommended practices:

Communication Encryption:

Utilize encryption protocols such as SSL/TLS to secure communications between users and servers. This ensures that exchanged data is encrypted and cannot be intercepted or modified by an attacker.

Strong Authentication:

Implement strong authentication for accessing sensitive systems and services. Use methods such as complex passwords, biometrics, authentication tokens, or digital certificates to enhance user identification.

Valid SSL/TLS Certificates:

Ensure that SSL/TLS certificates used to secure connections are valid and issued by trusted authorities. This ensures that communications are not compromised by forged certificates.

Server Identity Verification:

Before connecting to a server, verify its identity using certificates and digital signatures. Do not connect to a server whose identity cannot be verified.

Avoid Unsecured Public Wi-Fi:

Discourage employees from using unsecured public Wi-Fi networks to connect to company or organizational collborative applications. Prioritize the systematic use of Virtual Private Networks (VPNs) to secure connections when using public Wi-Fi networks.

Regular Software and System Updates:

Keep your software and systems up to date with the latest security patches. Regular updates help address known vulnerabilities and enhance the overall security of your systems.

In addition to these technical measures, user awareness training on MITM attack risks is crucial. Users should be educated to recognize signs of a MITM attack and adopt good cybersecurity practices, such as avoiding clicking on suspicious links or downloading unreliable files.

By following these best practices, you can enhance the security of your communications and minimize the risks of MITM attacks, ensuring the confidentiality and integrity of your data. Additionally, having cybersecurity insurance can provide coverage for damages related to cybercrime.

CHAPTER 1.10: RECOMMENDATIONS.

"Like a gentle breeze, sincere recommendation lights the way to the future."

Check-list for Physical Security related to Human Factors

Physical security, when considering the human factor, is crucial for safeguarding people, assets, and premises. A comprehensive check-list can contribute to strengthening these aspects. Here are some points to consider:

Access Control:

Implement secure access control systems, such as the use of access cards, PIN codes, or biometrics, to restrict entry to authorized personnel only.

Surveillance of Premises:

Install video surveillance systems in sensitive areas to deter undesirable behavior and monitor activities in real-time.

Security Training:

Conduct regular training sessions to raise employee awareness of physical security, including emergency evacuation procedures and secure access protocols.

Visitor Management:

Establish strict protocols for visitor management, including check-in procedures, issuance of temporary badges, and accompaniment by authorized personnel.

Equipment Protection:

Ensure that sensitive or expensive equipment is secure, with limited access granted only to authorized individuals.

Incident Response:

Develop incident response plans for physical incidents, such as intrusions, accidents, or other emergencies, to minimize risks.

Awareness of Social Threats:

Educate employees about risks associated with social engineering, including physical phishing, where individuals pose as legitimate employees to gain access to sensitive areas.

Security of IT Equipment:

Secure computers and electronic devices physically to prevent the theft of sensitive information.

Regular Assessment:

Conduct regular assessments of physical security to identify potential vulnerabilities and implement improvements.

By integrating these elements into your security strategy, you enhance the physical protection of your organization while considering the human factor. A holistic approach that combines advanced technological systems with adequate awareness and training will contribute to creating a secure and resilient environment.

Mobile/Tablet Security Checklist:

1. System Updates:
   - Ensure that your devices are running the latest operating system version to benefit from security patches.
2. Trusted Applications:
   - Download apps only from reliable sources, such as official app stores.
3. App Management:
   - Remove unnecessary apps and regularly review permissions granted to the apps you use.
4. App Permissions:
   - Control and limit permissions granted to apps to protect your personal data.
5. Location Security:

- Disable location services when not needed and regularly clear location history.

6. Separate User Accounts:
   - Create separate user accounts on shared devices.

7. Gmail Security:
   - Enhance security for Gmail accounts linked to your devices by enabling two-step verification.

8. Sleep and Lock:
   - Set your screen to sleep and lock automatically after a period of inactivity.

9. Screen Privacy:
   - Use a physical privacy filter to restrict screen visibility from specific angles.

10. Camera Cover:
    - Physically block the camera with a cover when not in use.

11. Disable Unused Features:
    - Turn off features like voice commands or connectivity that you don't regularly use.

12. Forget WiFi Networks:
    - Remove saved WiFi networks you no longer use to prevent unauthorized connections.

13. Turn Off Sharing:
    - Disable sharing features that you don't regularly use.

14. Advanced Security Measures:

- Consider advanced security measures such as unauthorized access detection based on your expertise and needs.
- Ensuring the security of your mobile devices and tablets involves a combination of software updates, app management, and privacy settings. Implementing these measures will help protect your personal information and enhance overall device security.

PC :

1. System Updates: Keep your operating system up to date by installing the latest available version.
2. Disable Voice Commands: to prevent unauthorized access.
3. Turn off location services and regularly clear history to protect your privacy.
4. Control app permissions to limit access to data.
5. Use programs and apps from trusted sources to avoid malware.
6. Remove unnecessary apps to reduce potential security risks.
7. Create separate user accounts, especially on shared devices.
8. Delete unnecessary accounts associated with your device to reduce potential access points.
9. Protect your accounts connected to your device by enabling security measures like two-step verification.

10. Set your screen to sleep and lock automatically after a period of inactivity.
11. Use a physical privacy filter to prevent others from viewing your screen.
12. Physically block the camera with a cover when not in use.
13. Disable connectivity (Bluetooth, Wi-Fi) that you're not using to reduce vulnerabilities.
14. Disable file sharing and other features not regularly used.
15. Disable autoplay to have better control over multimedia content.
16. Turn off unnecessary privacy options, including targeted ads.
17. Enhance your security by using a firewall and a virtual private network (VPN).
18. Consider advanced actions such as stopping malicious code execution and detecting unauthorized access based on your digital expertise level.

Password Management Best Practices :

1. Verification of Password Compromise :
   - Regularly check for password compromises using appropriate tools and proactively update your credentials.
2. Avoid Common Password Strategies:
   - Avoid using common password strategies and opt for complex combinations to enhance the security of your accounts.
3. Use a Reliable Password Manager:

- Use a trusted password manager to securely store and organize your credentials.
4. Regular Database Backups:
   - Periodically backup your password manager's database to prevent data loss.
5. Memorize Secure Passwords:
   - Memorize a few secure passwords for situations where using the password manager is not possible or recommended.
6. Secure Storage of Backup Passwords:
   - If necessary, store some passwords or backup codes outside the primary password manager, ensuring secure protection.
7. Security Measures for Online Password Managers:
   - If using an online password manager, ensure it has robust security measures in place.
8. Secure Password Sharing:
   - When sharing passwords, do so securely, avoiding insecure communication channels.
9. Never Share Passwords via Email or Messages:
   - Never share your password in response to emails, messages, or calls, even if they seem legitimate.
10. Regular Password Changes:
    - Change your passwords regularly to enhance the security of your accounts.
11. Awareness of Surroundings:

- Be aware of your environment and individuals who might observe your actions while entering passwords.

12. Two-Factor Authentication (2FA or MFA):
    - Use two-factor authentication (2FA or MFA) to add an extra layer of security to your accounts.

13. Avoid Biometric Unlock Methods:
    - Avoid using fingerprint or facial recognition (biometrics) for increased security.

14. Secure Recovery Questions:
    - Prepare more secure recovery questions to prevent unauthorized access to your accounts.

15. Stay Informed with Additional Readings:
    - Keep yourself informed about the latest security practices in password management through additional readings.

Organisation

Importance of a Formal Communication Policy in Cyber-security

The most crucial aspect, saved for the end, is that an organization should have a formalized, up-to-date, and widely known communication policy. This policy needs to be developed considering cybersecurity standards and best practices. It should address aspects such as the use of communication devices, handling sensitive information, information sharing procedures, and individual responsibilities for security. Furthermore, the policy should be accessible to all members of the organization, regularly updated to reflect technological advancements and potential threats, and subject to regular training to raise awareness among employees regarding communication-related risks. Effective communication of this policy will contribute to reducing vulnerabilities related to human factors in the field of cybersecurity.

Key Points to Consider in Policy Drafting:

Awareness and Training:

Formal policy educates employees on cybersecurity best practices. Regular training covers sensitive information management, threat recognition, and secure use of technologies.

Access Management:

The policy defines access permissions, limiting employees to accessing only information necessary for their responsibilities, reducing risks related to unauthorized or excessive access.

External Communications Management:

It establishes protocols for communication with external entities, ensuring secure email usage, source verification before sharing information, etc.

Removable Media Management:

The policy may regulate the use of removable media (USB drives, external hard drives) to minimize the risks of spreading malware.

Monitoring and Auditing:

It outlines procedures for monitoring communications and security-related activities, allowing for audits to ensure compliance with security standards.

Incident Response:

The policy specifies steps to follow in the event of a security incident, including notification, isolating affected systems, data recovery, and post-incident analysis.

Establishment of Responsibilities:

It clarifies everyone's responsibilities in terms of cybersecurity, crucial for creating an environment of shared accountability.

Regular Updates:

The policy must be regularly updated to remain relevant in the face of evolving threats and technologies.

In summary, a well-crafted communication policy fosters a culture of security within the organization, thereby reducing risks associated with human factors in the field of cybersecurity.

CHAPTER 1.11: CYBERSECURITY & AI

"The machine can imitate, but only humanity can innovate."

The Growing Threat of AI Misuse in Cybersecurity

The misuse of artificial intelligence (AI) for malicious purposes is becoming an increasingly significant concern. Here are some examples of how AI can be exploited for malicious activities:

Intelligent Adversarial Attacks:

cybercriminals can use AI to create automated attack systems capable of analyzing defense systems, identifying vulnerabilities, and adapting in real-time to bypass security measures.

Deepfakes and Image Manipulation: AI can be employed to generate manipulated multimedia content, such as deepfake videos or altered images, to spread false information, conduct disinformation campaigns, or compromise the reputation of individuals or organizations.

Enhanced Phishing and Social Engineering Attacks:

AI can generate more sophisticated phishing attacks by analyzing personal data available online, making phishing emails or messages more credible and harder to detect.

Botnets and Distributed Attacks:

Cybercriminals can use AI-controlled networks of infected machines, known as botnets, to carry out coordinated attacks, such as Distributed Denial of Service (DDoS) attacks, which can paralyze websites and online services.

Automatic Target Recognition:

AI can analyze large amounts of personal data to identify potential targets for targeted attacks, such as vulnerable businesses or individuals with sensitive information.

Attack Automation:

AI can automate certain stages of cyberattacks, such as spamming, malware propagation, or phishing attacks, allowing cybercriminals to conduct large-scale attacks with increased efficiency.

Evasion of Detection Techniques:

Cybercriminals can use AI to create malware capable of bypassing traditional rule-based detection systems. AI can generate variants of malware that are more challenging to detect.

Advanced Social Engineering:

AI can analyze extensive data on individuals, such as social media profiles, to create personalized social engineering attacks. This can make phishing or manipulation attacks more persuasive and deceive more people.

Vulnerability Detection Escalation:

AI can be used to analyze computer systems for vulnerabilities, helping cybercriminals identify weaknesses and plan more sophisticated attacks.

Targeted and Automated Attacks:

AI can gather information about a specific target, such as browsing habits, preferences, or online interactions. This information can then be used to personalize attacks and maximize their chances of success.

To counter these malicious uses of AI, it is crucial to strengthen security measures and develop advanced detection techniques. Close collaboration between researchers, industry, governments, and law enforcement agencies is essential to address these challenges and protect computer systems from cyberattacks.

Incorporating Intelligent SOC for Enhanced Security

To complement the security architecture discussed in this part of the course, it is essential to integrate an intelligent

Security Operations Center (SOC). By leveraging automation through an Artificial Intelligence (AI) platform like AITEK, the SOC becomes intelligent, offering advanced protection against cyber threats while reducing risks associated with human factors. This is a key element for a robust and proactive security architecture.

This concludes the first part of this handbook. The second part will delve into further strategies and technologies to enhance cybersecurity in the ever-evolving landscape of threats and technologies.

PART 2:
THE AI SOC

"Careful supervision reveals hidden weaknesses and paves the way for improvement."

CHAPTER 2.0: WHY USE AN SOC

"The why is the quest for meaning, the how is the path to realization."

Importance of a Security Operations Center (SoC)

A Security Operations Center (SoC) plays a crucial role in the fight against cybercrime. Here's why having a SoC is important:

Early Detection of Cyber Attacks:

The SoC uses advanced threat detection tools to continuously monitor activities on networks and computer systems. This enables early detection of cyber attacks, essential for minimizing damage and taking prompt remedial actions.

Security Incident Analysis:

The SoC analyzes security incidents and suspicious events to understand the tactics, techniques, and procedures used by cybercriminals. In-depth analysis enhances comprehension of attackers' motivations and methods, facilitating the implementation of appropriate security measures to counter their activities.

Rapid and Effective Incident Response:

Organizations with a SoC can react quickly and effectively to security incidents. The SoC has established procedures and protocols for incident management, allowing a coordinated and structured response. This helps limit damage, isolate compromised systems, and prevent the spread of attacks.

Continuous Security Monitoring:

A SoC ensures continuous monitoring of network and computer system security. This helps detect new threats and emerging vulnerabilities, allowing for preventive measures to strengthen security and protect digital assets.

Threat Intelligence Collection and Analysis:

The SoC collects and analyzes threat intelligence from various sources, both internal and external. This information enhances understanding of the threat landscape and anticipates potential attacks. It also helps identify attack patterns and trends, enabling proactive defense measures.

Continuous Security Improvement:

Through monitoring and analysis of security activities, a SoC enables continuous improvement of security measures. Lessons learned from past incidents and security events help identify gaps and implement corrective measures to enhance the organization's resilience against cyber threats.

In summary, having a SoC is essential in combating cybercrime as it allows for early detection of attacks, rapid incident response, continuous security monitoring, collection and analysis of threat intelligence, and continuous improvement of security measures. By investing in a SoC, organizations strengthen their ability to protect digital assets and respond to constantly evolving cyber threats.

Components of a Security Operations Center (SoC)

A Security Operations Center (SoC) is responsible for monitoring, detecting, analyzing, and responding to cybersecurity incidents within an organization. Here are the key components of a SoC:

Personnel:

The SoC includes a team of cybersecurity professionals such as security analysts, security engineers, threat intelligence experts, incident response specialists, etc. These experts monitor security activities, analyze incidents, take measures to mitigate risks, and coordinate incident responses.

Tools and Technologies:

A SoC employs various tools and technologies to monitor the organization's networks, systems, and applications. This may include Intrusion Detection Systems (IDS), Intrusion Prevention Systems (IPS), Security Information and Event Management (SIEM) systems, network monitoring tools, threat analysis tools, etc. These tools help collect and analyze security data, detect suspicious activities, and generate alerts for incidents.

Continuous Monitoring:

The SoC ensures continuous monitoring of the organization's security environment. This involves real-time collection and analysis of event logs, network data flows, security alerts, activity reports, etc. Continuous monitoring helps detect ab-normal activities, intrusion attempts, malware, and other potential threats.

Incident Detection and Analysis:

When a security incident is detected, the SoC conducts in-depth analysis to understand the nature of the incident, its potential impact, and the actions required for remediation. This may involve reviewing event logs, analyzing malware signatures, correlating alert data, investigating suspicious activities, etc. The goal is to identify the source of the incident, determine its scope, and take appropriate actions to mitigate risks.

Incident Response:

The SoC is responsible for coordinating and managing incident response. This includes implementing response plans, mobilizing necessary resources, coordinating remediation actions, restoring affected systems, and minimizing impacts. Incident response may also involve collaboration with internal or external teams, such as IT support teams, security service providers, law enforcement agencies, etc.

Reporting and Documentation:

The SoC generates reports and documents security activities, detected incidents, actions taken, and lessons learned. These reports are essential for evaluating the effectiveness of security measures, communicating with management and stakeholders, providing improvement recommendations, and meeting compliance and regulatory requirements.

In summary, a SoC comprises a team of cybersecurity experts, monitoring tools and technologies, mechanisms for incident detection and analysis, incident response processes, and reporting and documentation. Together, these components enable the SoC to monitor, detect, and respond to cyber-security incidents, protecting digital assets and preventing cybercrime.

CHAPTER 2.1: THREAT AND ACTIVE SURVEILLANCE

"Look at the sky even before the rain starts to fall."

Threat hunting is an advanced and essential practice in the field of cybersecurity. It involves the proactive identification of potential threats and the implementation of preventive measures to reduce risks. This process relies on hypotheses based on technical intelligence and specific threats that could target your organization.

A threat hunting exercise is not limited to a single approach, as cyberattacks are constantly evolving. It requires an experienced intervention team specialized in threat hunting, capable of acting quickly in case of an incident. This team adjusts its methods based on current threat data and information, allowing it to proactively target and eliminate potential threats.

One of the key benefits of threat hunting is its ability to identify threats exploiting weaknesses and vulnerabilities in cyberspace. By specifically addressing these threats, organizations can strengthen their security and protect sensitive systems and data. This is particularly crucial for nation-states, as cybersecurity plays a pivotal role in defending their national interests.

Establishing a threat hunting capability within a Security Operations Center (SoC) can significantly enhance a country's security. By responding quickly and effectively to cyber threats at both national and international levels, the country strengthens its cybersecurity position and protects critical infrastructure, sensitive data, and strategic resources.

Threat hunting also provides access to valuable intelligence across various data categories, including information on internet traffic, networks infected with malware, communications of cybercriminals, DNS/SMTP/Web intelligence, indicators of compromise (IoC), device information and behaviour, as well as activities on the dark web.

In summary, threat hunting is a crucial process to prevent cyberattacks and safeguard organizational systems and data. By investing in this practice, every state and enterprise must bolster its cybersecurity posture and enhance its capabilities to address emerging threats in the ever-evolving digital world.

Active monitoring is a key element to enhance the effectiveness of a Security Operations Center (SoC). It enables the SoC to undertake "Cyber Offense Operations," providing advanced capabilities for real-time monitoring and manipulation of IP traffic.

SoC operators can use active monitoring to directly interact with IP traffic, allowing them to redirect data, intercept communications, and modify the content of user data within the network. This capability of IP traffic data manipulation provides a comprehensive view of each user's activities, including interactions, frequency, and duration of communications.

One of the main advantages of active monitoring is its effectiveness in responding to threats such as terrorism. By actively monitoring communications and manipulating IP traffic data, the SoC can detect and prevent potential malicious activities, thereby protecting the country's sensitive data and highly confidential or classified information.

Key features of an active monitoring system include:

Packet Manipulation: The ability to modify and control data packets in real-time as they traverse a network. This functionality can be used for legitimate purposes such as optimizing network traffic, managing priorities, or implementing security policies. However, it also presents security risks when used maliciously.

Interception Triggers: The capability to define criteria that trigger the interception of network traffic based on pre-defined parameters. This includes criteria such as source or destination IP addresses, MAC addresses, specific keywords, and suspicious behaviours.

To mitigate risks associated with packet manipulation, it is crucial to implement appropriate security measures. This includes using encryption techniques to protect data integrity in transit, implementing strict filtering rules to allow only legitimate traffic, and conducting thorough inspection of network traffic using advanced intrusion detection systems.

Furthermore, continuous monitoring of network traffic is essential to identify any suspicious activity or attempted packet manipulation. The implementation of an anomaly detection system can help spot abnormal behaviours and trigger alerts in case of suspicious activity.

In summary, packet manipulation allows real-time modification and control of data packets. While it can be used legitimately to optimize the network, it also poses security risks. Therefore, implementing appropriate security measures, such as encryption, strict filtering rules, and active network traffic monitoring, is essential.

Interception Triggers: These refer to the ability to define criteria that trigger the interception of network traffic based on specific predefined parameters. These criteria can include source or destination IP addresses, MAC addresses, specific keywords, protocols such as RADIUS, DHCP, or VoIP, as well as suspicious behaviours.

The interception of network traffic can serve security, monitoring, or network management purposes. For example, an intrusion detection system can be configured to intercept and analyze traffic from a suspicious IP address to identify any malicious activity. Similarly, a network monitoring tool can be used to intercept traffic containing specific keywords related to potential threats.

However, the use of interception triggers also presents potential risks and impacts. Firstly, it is crucial to ensure that interception criteria are well-defined and relevant to avoid unnecessary or excessive interceptions, which could lead to privacy intrusions.

Additionally, it is essential to guarantee the confidentiality and security of intercepted data. Sensitive or confidential information intercepted must be protected against unauthorized access and securely stored. Encryption and data protection measures should be implemented to ensure the integrity and confidentiality of intercepted information.

Finally, it is important to note that the interception of network traffic must be conducted in compliance with applicable laws and regulations. Many countries have laws governing the interception of network traffic, and compliance with these regulations is essential to avoid violating user rights or facing legal issues.

In summary, interception triggers enable the definition of criteria to specifically target network traffic based on IP addresses, MAC addresses, keywords, specific protocols, or suspicious behaviours. While allowing detailed analysis of the corresponding traffic, careful configuration, data protection measures, and compliance with laws and regulations are necessary to mitigate potential risks.

Traffic Recording with Intelligent Storage: This feature allows the efficient storage and management of large amounts of traffic data for later analysis. It is essential for capturing and retaining network traffic data, which can be used for various analyses, particularly in the field of cybersecurity.

Traffic recording involves collecting all communication data traversing the network, including data packets, metadata, and other relevant information. These data are then stored in a data lake, a large-scale data storage structure that allows efficient and scalable data management.

Once recorded, the data can be analyzed using auto-ML platforms like Aitek. These platforms use machine learning techniques to analyze traffic data, detect patterns and anomalies, and generate insights and recommendations. Auto-ML automates part of the analysis process, reducing the need for human intervention and speeding up data processing time.

The advantage of using Aitek-type auto-ML platforms lies in their ability to efficiently process large amounts of traffic data, quickly identify complex patterns, and provide actionable results. These platforms are designed to adapt to specific cybersecurity needs, enabling threat detection, analysis of suspicious behaviors, and real-time alert generation.

In summary, recording traffic with intelligent storage allows the efficient storage and management of network traffic data for later analysis. Aitek-type auto-ML platforms facilitate the analysis of recorded data, providing insights and recommendations to enhance cybersecurity. This combination of traffic recording and analysis contributes to the early detection of threats and informed decision-making to protect systems and data from cybercrime.

Passive Network Topology Discovery: The ability to map and understand the structure and configuration of the network without disrupting its normal operation.

In summary, active monitoring plays a crucial role in protecting a country's infrastructure and sensitive information. By using advanced techniques for monitoring and manipulating IP traffic, SoCs can detect threats, prevent attacks, and ensure the security and integrity of the country's data:

CHAPTER 2.2: FUNCTIONAL TABLE

"A well-structured organization is like a precise clock, where each gear finds its place and contributes to the smooth running of the whole."

	FUNCTIONAL NEEDS	MARKET SOLUTIONS CAPABILITIES	SOLUTION FUNCTIONALITIES
1	Vulnerability Analysis, Resource Access, Exploits	- Information collection and alerting from a compromise indicators list - Watch analytic - Cloud Analytic Server - Detection of exploits used on resources from a predefined compromise indicators list	- Information and statistics collection on exploit usage and resource access - Packet Forensic (M1G4 or AiteK IoT or ITrade24)
2	Location of social media publications	- Collection and storage of social media content data	- Observation and recording of social media publications and activities - Packet Forensic (OU or AiteK IoT or ITrade24)
3	Encrypted VOIP Communication Interception	- Interception and processing of exchanges using standard VOIP protocols - Packet capture or interception, detailed call records and/or audio files recording - Decryption of encrypted contents using a valid PKI	- Interception, interpretation, and recording of encrypted VOIP communications - Packet Forensic (M1G4 or AiteK IoT or IVoice24 or Watch analytic or Cloud Analytic Server)
4	Packet-Level Manipulation	- Packet manipulation through techniques like "Man-in-the-middle," "Man-on-the-side" - Decryption of encrypted contents using a valid PKI	- Manipulation of network traffic data packets - Packet Forensic (M1G4 or AiteK IoT or Foren24)
5	Triggering Interceptions Based on Criteria	- Interception and alerts based on specific information such as IP, MAC address, keywords, RADIUS, DHCP, VOIP calls, and other criteria	- Detection and alerting based on specific criteria - Packet Forensic (M1G4 or Foren24)
6	Traffic Recording with Intelligent Buffering	- Recording and storage of all network traffic	- Storage and management of network traffic - Packet Forensic (M1G4 or Foren24)

	FUNCTIONAL NEEDS	MARKET SOLUTIONS CAPABILITIES	SOLUTION FUNCTIONALITIES
7	Passive Network Topology Discovery	- Extraction of metadata on network traffic	- Collection of information for network topology mapping - Packet Forensic (M1G4 or Foren24)
8	Collection and Analysis of Compromise Indicators	- Collection, logging, and alerting in the presence of specific compromise indicators	- Collection, recording, and alerting of compromise indicators - Same as in 1.
9	Interface with Third-Party Systems via APIs	- Storage of collected information in various standard formats - Integration of images in a web-based user interface	- Provision of data in industry-standard formats - Packet Forensic (M1G4 or Foren24)
10	Online Monitoring of Physical Environment	- Monitoring temperature, humidity, floods, smoke, airflow at room entrance - Tracking wireless devices with alerting capabilities	- Monitoring of the physical environment - Packet Forensic (5ENVSensor or Foren24) or AiteK IoT
12	Remote Management and Configuration Interface	- Remote system management and configuration via a graphical user interface, command-line interface, or text mode - Automatic remote OS and application updates	- Remote system management and configuration - Packet Forensic (M1G4 or Foren24) or C2 Master Server or Management

Please note that the tools mentioned above represent standard functionalities and must be tailored to meet the specific needs of clients, whether they are governmental or private.

CHAPTER 2.3: INTELLIGENT SOC ARCHITECTURE

"Vision without intelligence is blind, but intelligence without vision is sterile."

In the proposed centralized deployment architecture, three main components are deployed: the Master Server, the Configuration Agent (installed on the "probe" devices), and the Capture Rules Editor (Policy Editor). These components communicate with each other through a secure channel using the "peer-talk" tunneling protocol.

The Master Server, also known as the Master Server, is a process that can be executed locally on the probes or installed on a dedicated server. In the latter case, it will be installed on a separate server in a virtual machine. The Master Server is always active and accessible to analysts with an account. Its role is to define the environment or network perimeter in which the probe operates, manage capture rules, and securely store the collected data.

The Configuration Agent is deployed on each probe device, responsible for receiving directives from the Master Server regarding specific capture rules to apply. The Configuration Agent ensures that the probes operate in accordance with the parameters set by the Master Server.

The Capture Rules Editor, or Policy Editor, is an interface that allows analysts to adjust and customize capture rules based on the specific needs of the ongoing investigation or analysis. This editor facilitates the modification of capture parameters without requiring direct intervention on the probes.

Communication between these components occurs securely through a channel using the "peer-talk" tunneling protocol. This protocol ensures the confidentiality and integrity of exchanges between the Master Server, Configuration Agents, and Capture Rules Editor.

In summary, in this centralized architecture, the Master Server defines capture parameters and manages the network environment, Configuration Agents apply these directives on probes, and the Capture Rules Editor allows analysts to adjust rules based on specific needs, all ensuring secure communication between components through the "peer-talk" protocol.

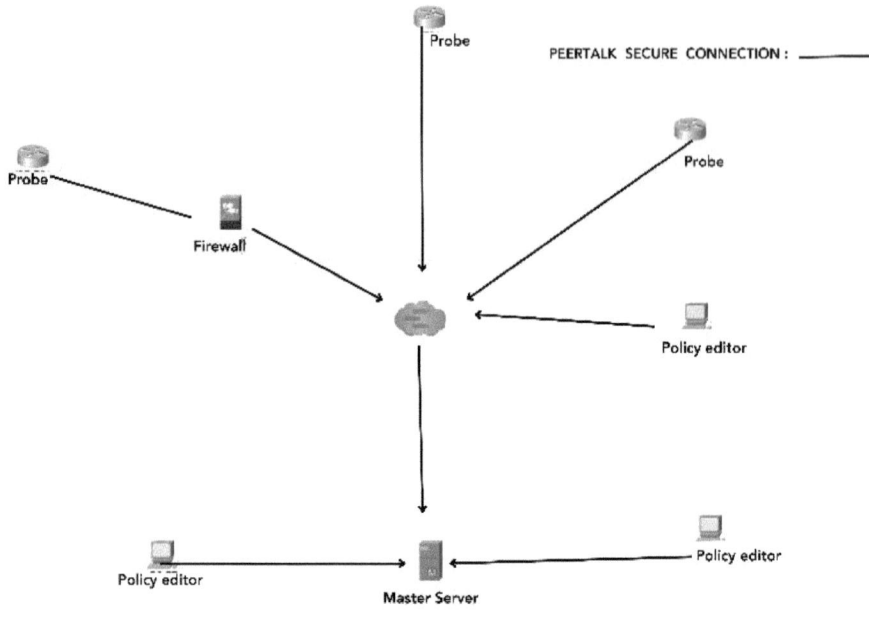

The Configuration Agent serves as a direct communication link with the Master Server. It facilitates communication between the probes and the Master Server, ensuring the collection and transmission of relevant data.

The Capture Rules Editor, also known as the Policy Editor, is a graphical interface that allows analysts to define and edit specific capture rules. It simplifies the configuration and customization of capture parameters based on specific needs.

Advancements in artificial intelligence have led to platforms such as Aitek SoC V6, offering advanced security policy management. This groundbreaking solution enables

the creation, modification, and supervision of rules, strategies, and security parameters within the SOC. Notably, it
includes dynamically adjusting configurations to align with
emerging threats.

One of the platform's strengths lies in its integrated knowledge cartridge, acting as a supervisor for proactive security
policy management. It allows intelligent adaptation based
on circumstances, fully leveraging the artificial intelligence
and machine learning features of Aitek V6. This real-time
adaptability enables more precise detection of security
incidents and a faster, more accurate response while automatically adjusting parameters to address new threats.

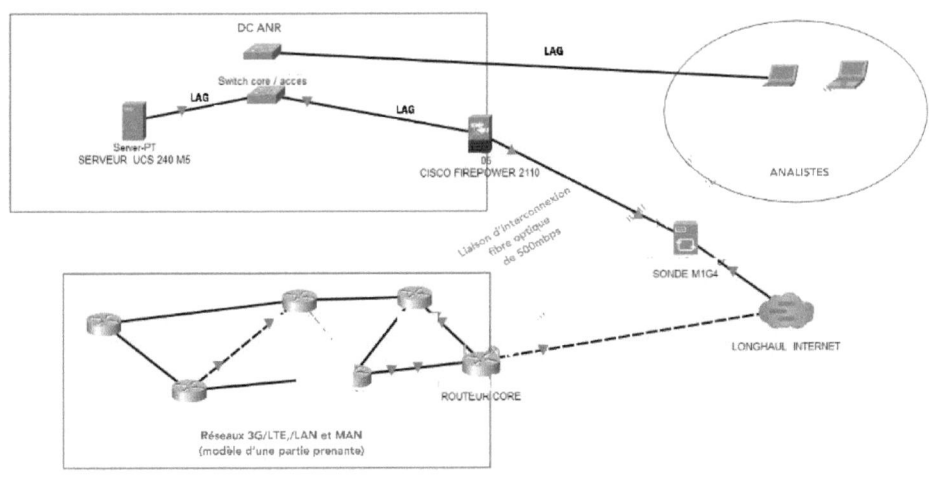

To ensure secure connectivity between the Internet edge devices of stakeholders, especially in sites with constraints and no direct link, an interconnection via the Internet is necessary. Implementing a secure tunnel between Internet edge devices such as routers and firewalls of stakeholders is recommended. This ensures the confidentiality and integrity of the exchanged data.

This centralized deployment architecture efficiently manages the probes and collects necessary data while ensuring secure communications.

In the detailed deployment architecture of probes for a stakeholder, each site will be interconnected with a set of M1G4 or AiteK IoT Foren24 probes in redundancy for threat hunting and active monitoring. The connection between sites will be established via a fiber optic link offering a throughput of 500 Mbps.

The deployment architecture at a site (stakeholder) is illustrated in the figure. A data center will host all the application solutions on virtual machines from the CISCO UCS 2440 M5 hypervisor or the Aitek SoC V6 knowledge cartridge. At each stakeholder's site, M1G4 or AiteK IoT Foren24 probes will be deployed and interconnected to the data center via dedicated fiber optic links with a minimum capacity of 500 Mbps.

The probes will be strategically positioned to intercept international outbound flows (Internet) from stakeholders, providing comprehensive visibility into international traffic coming to or from these entities.

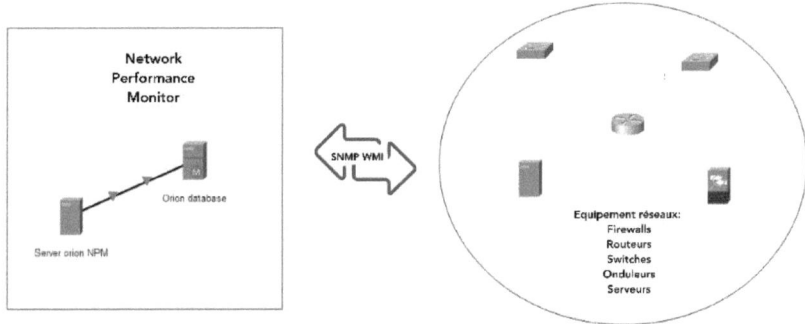

In this architecture, the components communicate with each other through a secure channel using the "peer-talk" tunneling protocol. The probes can collect data from various sources and formats. Here are the supported data formats by the probe:

- Packet Forensic - M1G4 or AiteK IoT Foren24
- Watch analytic or Aitek Cyber Supervisor
- Cloud Analytic Server or Aitek Cyber Supervisor
- Advanced Processing Key Software or Aitek Cyber Supervisor
- 5ENVSensor or AiteK IoT Foren24

These data formats enable the capture and analysis of different types of data streams to detect threats and monitor network activities.

As part of the component, a network of sites will be interconnected. Each site will be equipped with two (02) probes of the M1G4 or AiteK IoT Foren24 type in redundancy, specifically designed for threat hunting and active monitoring. The goal of these probes will be to detect and analyze potential threats to ensure the security of systems and data.

To ensure effective connectivity between sites, a fiber optic link will be established, providing sufficient throughput capacity. This fast and reliable interconnection will enable smooth communication between different sites and facilitate information sharing between probes.

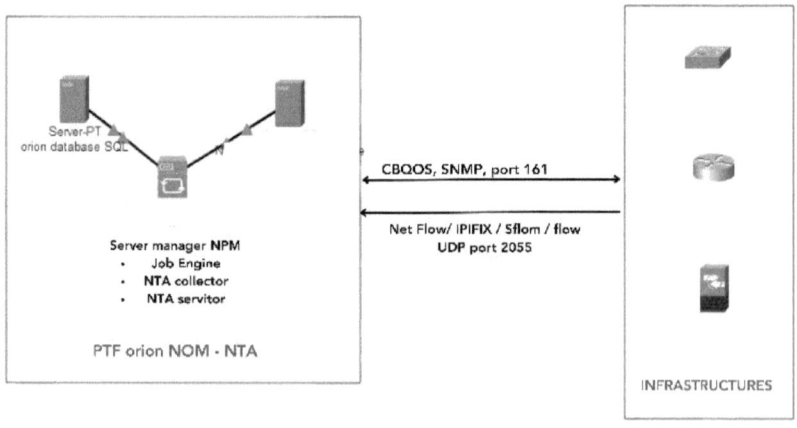

The deployment architecture for each site, dedicated to a stakeholder, is represented in the Figure: deployment architecture of probes for a stakeholder. In this architecture, the Datacenter will play a central role by hosting all the necessary application solutions. The solutions will run on virtual machines hosted by the CISCO UCS 2440 M5 hypervisor. This will allow efficient resource management and flexibility in application deployment.

At the level of each stakeholder, M1G4 or AiteK IoT Foren24 probes will be deployed and interconnected to the Datacenter via dedicated fiber optic links with a capacity of 500 Mbps. This setup ensures precise data collection and proactive traffic monitoring. The probes will be strategically positioned to intercept international outbound flows of the stakeholders, thus providing complete visibility over both incoming and outgoing international traffic.

To ensure the confidentiality and integrity of the exchanged data, all components of the architecture will communicate through a secure channel based on the network tunneling protocol. This technique encapsulates and transports data from one network through another network. It creates a secure and private "tunnel" within a public or another network, enabling confidential data transmission.

The principle of tunneling involves encapsulating data packets of one protocol within another protocol to transport them securely. When a packet is encapsulated, it becomes the "payload" of the tunneling protocol and is routed through the destination network.

Tunneling protocol can be used in various scenarios, such as secure remote access (VPN), firewall traversal, connecting distant local area networks (LAN), or routing traffic through public networks like the Internet.

Commonly used tunneling protocols include IPsec (Internet Protocol Security), L2TP (Layer 2 Tunneling Protocol), PPTP (Point-to-Point Tunneling Protocol), GRE (Generic Routing Encapsulation), and SSH (Secure Shell) for secure tunneling.

The network tunneling protocol ensures secure and private data transport across a network by encapsulating data packets within another protocol. This offers protection against interceptions and enables transparent communication between distant networks.

This protocol will ensure secure exchanges protected against attempts to intercept or manipulate data.

In addition to their monitoring role, the probes will also be capable of collecting data from various sources and formats. They will support a variety of data formats such as SQL, Redis, Office, MongoDB, and many others. This flexibility will provide a comprehensive and detailed view of traffic and activities within the stakeholder environments.

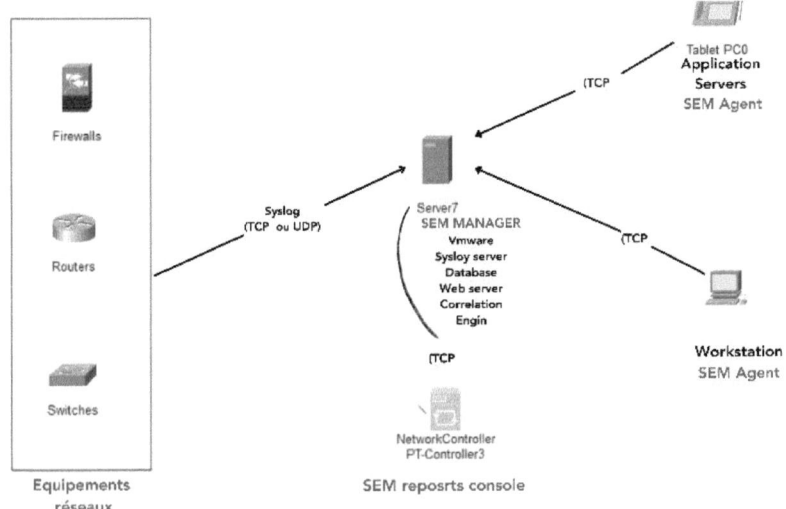

Firewalls

Routers

Switches

Equipements
réseaux

Syslog
(TCP ou UDP)

Server7
SEM MANAGER
Vmware
Sysloy server
Database
Web server
Correlation
Engin

(TCP

NetworkController
PT-Controller3

SEM reposrts console

Tablet PC0
Application
Servers
SEM Agent

(TCP

(TCP

Workstation
SEM Agent

In summary, the detailed probe deployment architecture for a stakeholder will guarantee advanced surveillance, proactive threat detection, and a deep understanding of international traffic. This will enhance security measures and enable stakeholders to make informed decisions to prevent incidents and protect their systems and data.

The detailed architecture of the Security Operations Center (SoC) core infrastructure serves as a model, demonstrating how various components are interconnected, A graphic representation of this architecture is shown in the figure.. It's important to note that the components mentioned are examples, and equivalent components from other manufacturers like Nokia, Huawei, etc., can also be used.

Central to this architecture is a physical server, for instance, the CISCO UCS C240 M5, chosen here as an example. On this server, virtual servers will be deployed for various SoC solutions. However, similar servers from other brands can be utilized effectively.

For network connectivity and high availability, the model includes two switches, like the CISCO C9500 16x. These are installed in redundancy but could be substituted with equivalent switches from Nokia, Huawei, or other reputable manufacturers.

The CISCO Firepower 2110 is suggested for managing communication permissions between the infrastructure's core and the probes. Nevertheless, similar devices from different manufacturers can be employed to fulfill the same role, ensuring efficient permission management and enhanced security.

The proposed hardware components, such as 800 GB NVMe SSDs, 2 TB SATA hard drives, and CISCO Catalyst 9500 network cards, are specific choices. Equivalent components with similar specifications from Nokia, Huawei, or other brands can also be integrated into the architecture.

In essence, while the architecture is detailed with specific products, it is designed to be flexible, accommodating equivalent components from various manufacturers. This flexibility allows for customization based on availability, cost, and compatibility, ensuring that the SoC can meet the security needs of stakeholders and maintain a secure, threat-protected environment.

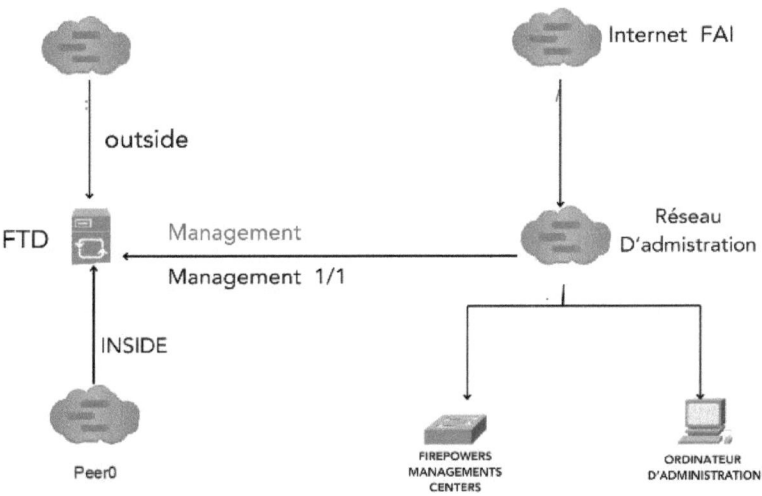

CHAPTER 2.4: MARKET TOOLS

"A good craftsman always knows his tools."

Choosing a solution like SolarWinds or the Aitek Soc V6 supervisor, which is indeed a major player in the market for supervision, is crucial. Their Orion platform offers a comprehensive range of products for network monitoring, security, and IT infrastructure administration. These products are designed to be powerful yet user-friendly, operating on a common technological platform, like the Solar-Winds Orion or the Aitek Soc V6 supervisor. This setup allows for individual implementation and expansion based on the specific needs of each company.

The supervisor platform, whether it's Aitek Soc V6 or Orion, combines network and operating system performance data from multiple elements of the tech stack to provide a unified view of the infrastructure's health. It's easy to install and configure and adapts to networks of all sizes. Administrators are equipped with robust tools to identify, isolate, diagnose, and quickly resolve network issues.

A key product of the Aitek Soc V6 or Orion-type platform is the Network Performance Monitor (NPM), a network monitoring solution offering numerous benefits. Key features include:

Network Availability Monitoring: NPM detects, isolates, and aids in resolving network performance issues.

Visualization of Critical Links: it quickly identifies issues in pathways to key applications or users, enhancing understanding of how the network delivers these applications.

Intelligent Network Mapping: solarWinds-type network mapping tools allow for easy creation of custom maps and visual packet paths.

Performance Analysis: NPM correlates performance data from multiple sources and data types, simplifying network performance issue resolution.

Advanced Alerts: network administrators are notified in real-time when defined health or performance thresholds are exceeded, enabling quick detection, diagnosis, and resolution of associated problems.

In addition to NPM, the Orion-type platform offers other essential tools for IT infrastructure administration, including:

SAM (Server Application Monitor): monitors applications and underlying infrastructure, whether on-premise, in the cloud, or in a hybrid environment.

NCM (Network Configuration Manager): manages configurations, changes, and compliance of routers, switches, and other network devices, saving time and improving network reliability and security.

VMAN (Virtualization Manager): monitors virtualization, manages performance, plans capacity, and optimizes VMware vSphere, Microsoft Hyper-V, and Nutanix AHV environments.

These complementary tools of the Orion-type platform offer advanced functionalities for efficient IT infrastructure administration, covering aspects like application monitoring, configuration management, and virtualization.

In summary, the Orion-type SolarWinds platform offers a complete solution for monitoring and managing IT infrastructure. It enables quick detection, diagnosis, and resolution of network performance and failure issues, while providing advanced tools for application monitoring, configuration management, and virtualization.

Aitek-type platforms with their IoT Box and "SoC" know-ledge cartridge can also be an interesting and more efficient alternative, as they integrate AI and intelligent agents that assist humans in supervision, anticipation, and correction (see the last chapter).

Resource Requirements: A SEM (Security Event Manager) platform continuously collects data from a fluctuating traffic flow depending on user, server, and network activity.

To ensure optimal functioning of the platform, the following resources are required:

SEM Manager Server:

- Processor: 8 vCPU
- Memory: 32 GB
- Storage: 2 TB
- Network Card: 1 GigaEthernet
- Reporting Server:
- Processor: 2 vCPU
- Memory: 4 GB

These hardware specifications are suitable for an environment comprising more than 1000 hosts. Installing a SIEM (Security Information and Event Management) plat-form like SEM is one of the most effective ways to prevent security incidents, detect threats, and help businesses comply with current regulations.

The Security Event Manager (SEM) is a vital component for any security platform. In the context of Aitek SoC V6, this functionality is natively integrated, meaning it is an inherent and fundamental part of the platform.

SEM is designed to monitor and analyze security events on the network in real-time. With Aitek SoC V6, this functionality is enriched with a machine learning engine. This means that the platform can autonomously identify and respond to security events, based on the analysis and understanding of behavior patterns.

The alarm capabilities allow the platform to signal critical or potentially dangerous events. It can also implement pre-defined or dynamic action plans in response to these events. These action plans may include automated measures to contain a threat, isolate parts of the network, or initiate remediation processes.

By integrating this functionality directly into Aitek SoC V6, it enhances the platform's ability to be proactive against threats, effectively respond to security events, and adapt to new forms of attacks thanks to its self-learning engine.

Cisco Duo MFA: cisco Duo Security is a dual-factor security solution offered by Cisco, helping businesses implement a "zero trust" security strategy inside and outside their network. This solution also meets companies' evolving expectations for personal data security.

Key benefits of Cisco Duo Security include: multi-Factor Authentication: Dual authentication verifies user identities before granting access

The management of the VMware Carbon Black Cloud Work-load solution is facilitated through a web-based console, accessible via browsers such as Google Chrome (current version and the two previous versions), Mozilla Firefox (current version and the two previous versions), and Microsoft Edge (current version and the two previous versions).

In computing, a workload refers to a specific computational task or set of tasks executed on a computer system or infrastructure. This could include processes, applications, tasks, or services running on a server, virtual machine, cloud, or any other computing environment.

Workloads encapsulate all tasks and activities a computing system must process and execute. This encompasses running applications, managing data, processing transactions, network communication, storage operations, and more. Workloads can vary in size, complexity, and resource requirements. Some are lightweight, requiring minimal resources, while others are more intensive, demanding significant computational, storage, and network capacities.

Virtualization and cloud computing technologies are commonly used to efficiently run and manage workloads, allowing dynamic allocation and management of resources based on the needs of each application or service.

Effective workload management is crucial to ensure efficient use of IT resources, optimal performance, service availability, and adherence to operational and security requirements. Security solutions like "VMware Carbon Black Cloud Workload" are designed to protect these workloads against threats and potential attacks.

The "VMware Carbon Black Cloud Workload" solution is based on an architecture that facilitates integration between "vCenter Server" and the "Carbon Black Cloud". This design enables seamless incorporation of the solution into the existing virtual environment.

The "VMware Carbon Black Cloud Workload" application is deployed within the virtual environment, directly onto the workloads that need protection. It acts as a security agent, collecting and transmitting relevant information about the activities and behaviors of the workloads to the "Carbon Black Cloud" platform.

Communication between the workloads and the "Carbon Black Cloud" platform is secure, utilizing robust encryption and authentication protocols. This ensures the confidentiality and integrity of the exchanged data and protection against compromise or interception attempts.

Once data is collected by the agent from the workloads, it is transmitted to the "Carbon Black Cloud" platform for real-time analysis. The platform employs advanced threat detection and behavioral analysis techniques to identify suspicious or malicious activities.

This architecture provides security teams with complete visibility into workload activities, even in complex and dynamic virtual environments. They can swiftly detect abnormal behaviors, ongoing attacks, or signs of compromise, enabling a quick and effective response to security incidents.

Thus, the "VMware Carbon Black Cloud Workload" solution employs an architecture that ensures secure communication between workloads and the "Carbon Black Cloud" platform. This architecture allows for real-time data collection, advanced threat analysis, and rapid response to security incidents in virtual environments. Like all the components proposed in our security architecture, it feeds our Intelligent SoC.

For optimal system availability and performance, it is recommended to have two servers for the role of Duo Proxy, and two load balancer servers to ensure system reliability and efficiency.

CHAPTER 2.5: THE AITEK6 SOC KNOWLEDGE CARTRIDGE

"Knowledge is the key to success."

The development of knowledge cartridges in AITEK-type solutions hinges on a collaborative effort between technical teams and the valuable industry expertise provided by clients and partners. This synergy facilitates the creation of a diverse range of knowledge cartridges tailored to various sectors and domains.

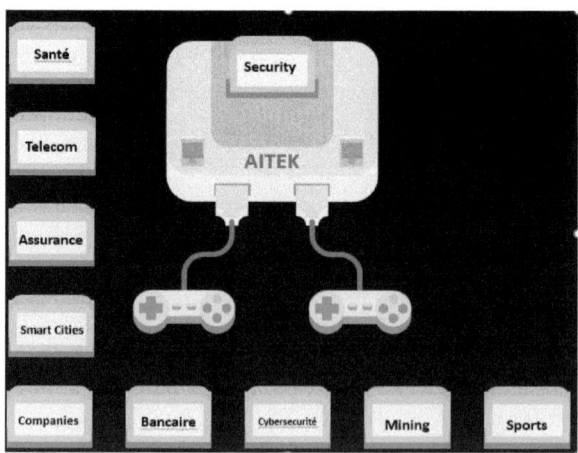

This capitalization has led to a significant collection of knowledge cartridges covering several industries. These cartridges have been meticulously crafted to address the unique challenges and requirements encountered in different industries. They encapsulate best practices, insights, and tailor-made solutions for each sector, refined through technical expertise and deep industry knowledge.

The current range of AITEK knowledge cartridges spans a broad spectrum of industries, ensuring that AITEK-type solutions are applicable and relevant to a variety of sectors, including healthcare, finance, manufacturing, retail, and many others. AITEK knowledge cartridges provide industry-specific guidance and ready-to-use components, facilitating the rapid implementation and optimization of solutions.

These knowledge cartridges are more than just data repositories; they represent a confluence of industry insights and practical solutions. Their diversity ensures that businesses across various sectors can leverage AITEK-type solutions to address specific challenges, enhance operational efficiency, and drive innovation. By continually updating and expanding these cartridges, AITEK stays at the forefront of industry trends and technological advancements, providing clients with cutting-edge tools and knowledge to maintain a competitive edge.

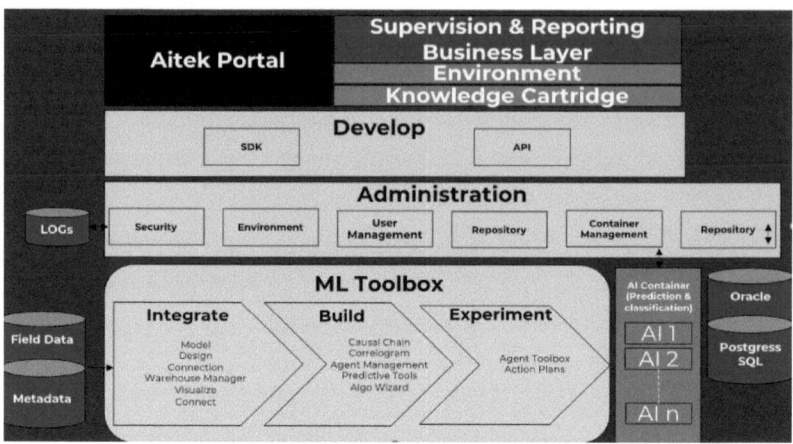

Each knowledge cartridge in the AITEK solution is designed to harness the power of the AITEK platform and tailor it to the unique characteristics and requirements of a specific sector. These cartridges incorporate pre-set configurations, algorithms, data models, and finely-tuned rules to meet the specific challenges and seize opportunities unique to each sector. They utilize the collective expertise and experiences of clients and partners to offer targeted solutions that enhance operational efficiency, facilitate decision-making, and uncover new perspectives in their respective industries.

The Aitek platform developer continues to expand and enrich its library of knowledge cartridges through ongoing collaboration with clients and partners. By combining technical know-how with specific industry knowledge, Aitek ensures its solutions remain at the forefront of innovation, enabling organizations to effectively leverage their industry expertise.

In summary, a knowledge cartridge in the AITEK solution is a powerful tool incorporating a complete semantic model tailored to operational units or specific domains. It includes predefined databases, agent libraries, operational unit configurations, alarms, predefined action plans, a semantic model (Knowledge Builder), customized dashboards, and an intelligent agent manager. These cartridges offer several advantages, including accelerated implementation, integration of industry best practices, customized solutions, improved data management and analysis, intelligent monitoring and alerting, customization options, and centralized management. These benefits contribute to enhancing operational efficiency, informed decision-making, and the ability to achieve meaningful results for organizations.

When implementing an Aitek-type knowledge cartridge for a SoC (Security Operations Center), it's important to consider objectives and risks related to the human factor. Here are some objectives to consider:

Security Awareness: the goal is to raise employee awareness of IT security risks, encouraging responsible behaviour and contributing to the organization's protection.

Training and Skills: essential to train security operations personnel to possess the skills needed to detect, analyze, and effectively respond to security incidents.

Threat Monitoring and Detection: the SoC must continuously monitor the network and systems, detect suspicious or malicious activities, and take appropriate countermeasures.

Incident Response: the aim is to have a well-defined incident response process for rapid and coordinated action in the event of a security incident, including incident management, evidence collection, and remediation.

Identity and Access Management: ensure rigorous management of identities and access to guarantee that only authorized persons have access to critical organizational resources.

Regulatory Compliance: ensure that security policies and practices comply with applicable regulations and standards to avoid legal and financial consequences.

Regarding human factor risks, it's essential to address them to ensure SoC effectiveness:

Human Errors: human errors can lead to security vulnerabilities and compromise data protection. Preventive measures and awareness are important to reduce these risks.

Insider Malice: malicious employees can pose a threat to organizational security. Proper access management and monitoring are necessary to detect and prevent malicious behavior.

Social Engineering: social engineering attacks often target employees by manipulating them to gain sensitive information. Proper security awareness training can help prevent these types of attacks.

<u>Negligenc</u>e: employee negligence can create security vulne-rabilities. Ongoing training and regular reminders about good security practices are necessary to minimize this risk.

In conclusion, establishing an intelligent SoC must consider human-related objectives, such as awareness, training, and incident response, as well as associated risks like human errors, insider malice, social engineering, and negligence. A holistic approach will strengthen the overall security of the organization.

An AI platform like Aitek integrating a SoC-type knowledge cartridge becomes an indispensable pivot to a modern SoC architecture.

CHAPTER 2.6: AI IN THE FIGHT AGAINST CYBERCRIME

"In digital mist, AI, vigilant guide, thwarts shadow of crime."

Artificial Intelligence (AI) can play a significant role in combating cybercriminals in various ways. Here's an expanded view of how AI can help counter cyber threats:

Threat Detection: AI can be leveraged to detect suspicious activities and malicious behaviors across networks. Utilizing machine learning techniques, AI can analyze vast amounts of data in real-time to identify patterns of cyberattacks and abnormal behaviors. This capability enables organizations to quickly identify attacks and take countermeasures. By constantly monitoring network traffic, AI algorithms can spot anomalies that may indicate a breach, such as unusual network traffic patterns or unexpected access requests.

Attack Prevention: AI can identify vulnerabilities in systems and networks and recommend preventative measures to rectify them. It can also help strengthen security mechanisms by analyzing traffic patterns and establishing early detection mechanisms to prevent attacks before they occur. AI systems can predict and thwart potential cyber-attacks by analyzing historical data and identifying trends that precede an attack.

Data Analysis: Cybercriminals often leave digital traces when they commit their crimes. AI can analyze vast amounts of data from various sources, such as event logs, login data, and surveillance data, to identify patterns and trends that might indicate suspicious activity. This deep data analysis can help prevent attacks and detect intrusions more rapidly. AI tools can sift through the noise to find the signal - identifying the real threats among a sea of data points.

Improving Intrusion Detection Systems (IDS): traditional IDS are often rule-based and can be circumvented by skilled attackers. AI can enhance these systems using machine learning techniques to learn to recognize normal and abnormal network traffic behaviors, thereby detecting sophisticated attacks that static rules cannot easily identify.

Incident Response: AI can also help automate the security incident response. By analyzing contextual information about an ongoing attack, AI can recommend appropriate measures to neutralize the threat, including implementing additional firewalls, blocking malicious IP addresses, or disabling compromised accounts. Automation of response allows for quick and effective action against cyberattacks.

It's crucial to note that while AI can be a valuable tool in the fight against cybercriminals, it cannot solve all security problems alone. A holistic approach, combining AI with other security measures such as user education, patch management, system hardening, and following best security practices, is necessary to effectively counter cyber-criminals.

In a Security Operations Center (SoC), AI plays a critical role in making it smarter and more efficient. Aitek-type plat-forms, with their IoT Box and knowledge cartridges, can certainly be an interesting alternative to enhance super-vision, anticipation, and correction of security threats in an IT environment. These platforms typically combine AI with intelligent agents to provide human assistance in managing security operations.

Benefits of these solutions include:

Enhanced Supervision: intelligent agents embedded in these platforms can continuously monitor systems and net-works, collecting real-time data to detect suspicious beha-viors or anomalies. They can analyze this data using AI techniques to identify potential threats and alert security teams, enabling proactive surveillance and early detection of security incidents.

Threat Anticipation: through AI and predictive analytics, Aitek platforms can anticipate threats by identifying pat-terns and early indicators associated with imminent attacks. Intelligent agents can alert security teams and recommend appropriate preventative measures to strengthen security posture before an attack occurs.

Automated Correction: intelligent agents can also assist security teams in incident remediation. Using knowledge previously stored in knowledge cartridges, they can recommend specific mitigation measures to resolve security issues, enabling faster and more effective incident response.

Resource Optimization: Aitek platforms allow for the optimization of human resources by automating routine tasks. Intelligent agents can perform security analyses, generate reports, and provide recommendations, thereby reducing the workload of security analysts. This enables teams to focus on more complex and strategic tasks.

Continuous Learning: Aitek platforms often use machine learning techniques to improve their capabilities over time. Intelligent agents can learn from new threats and tactics used by cybercriminals, adapting to changes in the cybersecurity landscape, thus enabling continuous improvement of detection and response capabilities.

APPENDIXES

Information Security - our services

OFFENSIVE SECURITY	GOVERNANCE & RISK MANAGEMENT	INFRASTRUCTURE SECURITY	COMPLIANCE	SOC CERT
Using cybercriminals' techniques	Organizing IS defense and risk management	Designing and deploying security infrastructures	Achieving, maintaining and demonstrating compliance	Detect and act against attacks
Intrusion testing · Black box · Grey box · White box · Red Team **Code audits** Configuration audits (on premise and public cloud) Architectural audits Reverse Engineering Social Engineering Technical expertise Forensic	ISS governance PSSI - Charter - Dashboard Definition and implementation of SSI processes **Risk analysis** **Awareness** - Phishing Support in implementing **security solutions** Organizational audits BIA, PCA, PRA, PSI, PRU **Cyber-Crisis** Management, Tests and Exercises **RSSI as a Service**	**Technical architecture design** · Security and network architecture: hosting, internet access, defense in depth · Authentication solution · Cloud and data security · IAM, IDaaS **Security project management:** calls for tender, solution selection, industrialization and deployment management **Operational safety:** technical expertise, N3 operations and support, continuous improvement	PCI DSS certification ARJEL certification PCI DSS, ARJEL, LPM, ASIP, ISO27001 **compliance** DCP: Mapping and RGPD compliance **Audit of compliance** with internal and sectoral standards **Extended enterprise** security: auditing service providers (TMA, outsourcing, SaaS, etc.)	SOC / CERT services Security incident response Managed internal and external security incident detection services **Protection services:** vulnerability scanning and management, EDR solutions management Tactical threat intelligence from our offensive activities Consulting and auditing in SOC / CSIRT organization **Security Rating:** a measure of cyber security maturity

AITEK-WATCH SOC & CERT managed services offer

IA Robot Managed services

Anticipation	Protection	Detection	Reaction

· Council cyber defense program
 	
· Threat intelligence and risk assessment with GRC experts
 	
· Phishing campaign
 	
· Safety awareness and crisis management exercises
 	
· Participation in redteam / purpleteam audit
 	
· Continuous assessment (Security Rating)
	· Vulnerability watch and managed vulnerability scanning
	
	· Optimization of solution security functions (WAF, IDS/IPS, EDR, XDR, etc.)
		· External vigilance services
		  · Detection of security events on your external technical assets
		  · Detecting usurpation of your legitimate assets
		  · Detection of exposure of sensitive information on the Internet
		
		· Internal attack detection services
		  · Log correlation monitoring and detection / SIEM
		  · Collection / centralization of logs on local or shared AITEK datalake
			· Intervention at CERT's request
			  · Major incident response
			  · Forensic
			  · Reverse engineering of malware
			  · Search for compromises
			  · Crisis management
			
			· Setting up and running dedicated internal CSIRTs
			
			· Automated response solutions

Increase the cost of an attack and break the economic logic of cybercriminals + manage internal malevolence

1. Identify corporate threats and feared events

2. Manage vulnerabilities to reduce the attack surface

3. Design a collection and detection strategy to manage security incidents as early as possible

4. Reduce the impact of proven security incidents

- Mapping of external assets (IPs, domains) and data marker keywords belonging to your organization
- Multi-source external data collection, automated enrichment and processing by vigilance modules
- Qualification of alerts by SOC AITEK-WATCH analysts

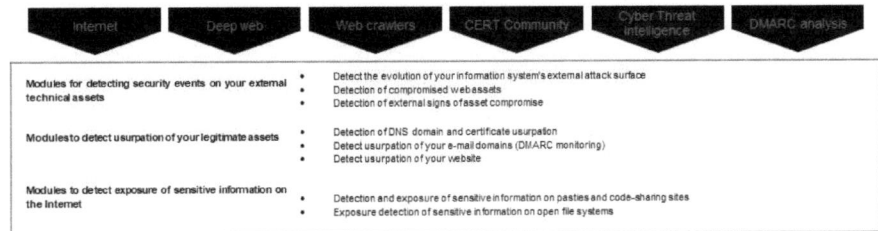

Internet	Deep web	Web crawlers	CERT Community	Cyber Threat intelligence	DMARC analysis

Modules for detecting security events on your external technical assets	• Detect the evolution of your information system's external attack surface • Detection of compromised web assets • Detection of external signs of asset compromise
Modules to detect usurpation of your legitimate assets	• Detection of DNS domain and certificate usurpation • Detect usurpation of your e-mail domains (DMARC monitoring) • Detect usurpation of your website
Modules to detect exposure of sensitive information on the Internet	• Detection and exposure of sensitive information on pasties and code-sharing sites • Exposure detection of sensitive information on open file systems

- Monitoring your internal information system by collecting and correlating logs

- Two possible AI PIPELINE collection architectures
  - Splunk Datalake on your information system (on premise or in the cloud)
  - Shared ELK datalake hosted by AITEK
  - Microsoft Sentinel Datalake & AI Module

- Detection strategy
  - Based on AITEK's usecase catalog + customized usecases via our AI
  - Leveraging the cyber threat intelligence gathered by the AITEK-WATCH SOC / CERT
  - Usecase factory for continuous improvement

- Service based on processing capacity, providing budget security and independence from data volumes

SOC reporting and ticketing portal :

Portal SOC AI PIPELINE

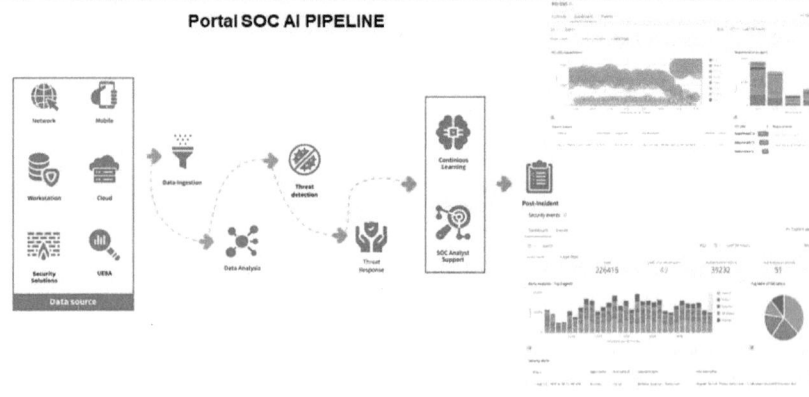

SOC Conceptual Architecture

Logging messages are considered the most useful data type to acquire. Logging messages summarize an action or an activity that took place on a system, containing information related to an associated event. Depending on your environment, you might want to consider collecting logging messages from various forms of security, network, and application products. Examples of physical and virtual devices that could provide valuable logging messages include the following:

Security elements such as firewalls, intrusion detection and prevention systems, antivirus solutions, web proxies, and malware analysis tools
Network elements such as routers, switches, and wireless access points and controllers
Operating systems such as the different releases of Microsoft Windows, UNIX, Linux, and OS X
Virtualization platforms such as Virtual-Box, Kernel-based Virtual Machine (KVM), Microsoft Hyper-V, and VMware ESX
Applications such as web servers, Domain Name System (DNS) servers, e-mail gateways, billing applications, voice gateways, and mobile device management (MDM) tools
Databases
Physical security elements such as security cameras, door access-control devices, and tracking systems
Systems used in process and control networks, such as supervisory control and data acquisition (SCADA) and distributed control system (DCS)

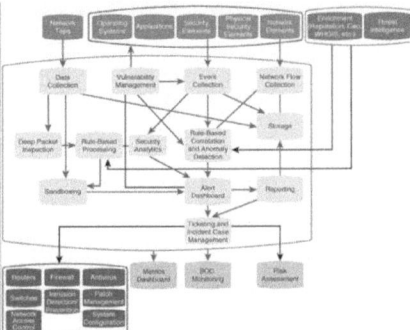

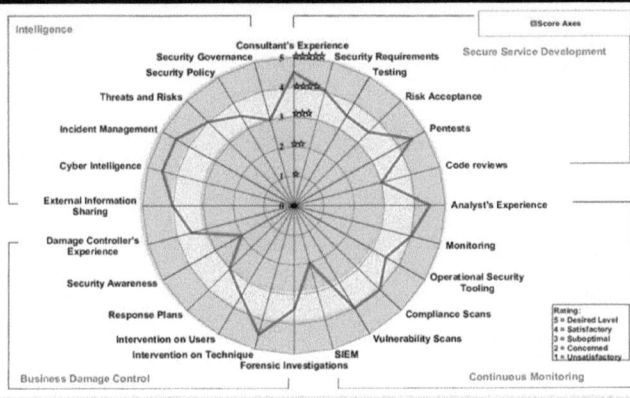

161

FOCUSED ON AI DEVELOPER BY THE FOUNDER

Our AI-powered SOC and API OPENAI is designed to give organizations a significant advantage in the fight against cybersecurity threats.

Integration of machine learning algorithms and predictive analytics into its operations.	Ability to identify and respond to potential threats with unprecedented speed and accuracy.
Detection and analysis of behavior patterns indicative of malicious activity.	Automate threat response processes to quickly neutralize potential threats.
Continuous learning from data and user feedback to improve detection capabilities over time.	Achieve a higher level of threat detection and response than traditional security methods can match.

Reduce SOC analyst fatigue and burnout by automating routine tasks, enabling analysts to concentrate on more complex threats and investigations.

Protection – Vulnerability management

View vulnerabilities in the SOC portal

- Vulnerability watch
- Managed vulnerability scanning
  - Qualifying vulnerabilities in your context
  - Provide you with the relevant information to prioritize your remedial actions

- Continuous monitoring with regular scans and differential work

- Focus on :
  - Assets exposed on the Internet / to third parties
  - Workstations
  - Servers directly exposed from workstations

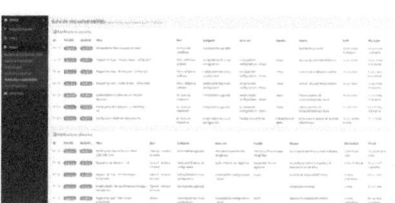

Our technology partner :

- CERT AITEK-WATCH responds to incidents for all companies, whether or not they are SOC customers.
- Implementation of a remote or on-site response system

| Triggering the service | Qualification telephone meeting | Proposal for an initial response system | Incident response operations | Hot feedback | Conclusion |

Containment actions to confine the incident or adversary and limit the possibility of compromising other assets

Eradication actions to remove a component of the attack

Hardening measures to prevent exploitation of a vulnerability

Remediation and return-to-normal actions

With AITEK GRC experts :
- Crisis management
- Internal and external communications
- Contractual and legal consequences

Raising your employees' awareness of the main attack vector: e-mail

> ### Customized campaigns

Example theme: internal competition
- To boost employee morale, your management team is offering a chance to win weather produced in conjunction with a partner (or any other object relevant to your business).

Example theme: internal survey on teleworking difficulties
- An internal survey has been carried out to identify problems and difficulties associated with employees' teleworking conditions.

Example topic: Data leakage from HRIS software
- Communication with users about an incident that led to the leakage of employee data from HRIS software.

Example topic: internal press release on COVID-19
- Internal press release to inform you of the new measures adopted by your company to ensure the survival of the group and limit the economic impact of the crisis.

> ### Credibility :
- Adapting the scenario to your business
- Use or mention of relevant contacts
- Use of a customized domain name
- Home page customization (logo, etc.)

> ### Campaign mechanics

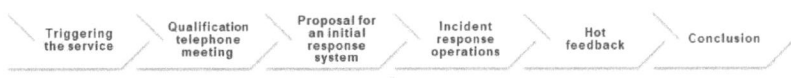

1. Receipt of a personalized phishing e-mail inviting you to connect to a website

2. Opening a link to a home page with an authentication form
   - 1st indicator: link open rate

3. Entering login information
   - 2nd Indicator: rate of data entry for identifiers

4. If the victim completes and submits the form, an error page is displayed.
   - The information entered is not stored.